D0946194

The Good C

THE
GOOD
CIGAR

H. PAUL JEFFERS
AND
KEVIN GORDON

With Illustrations by Kevin Gordon

BROADWAY BOOKS **NEW YORK**

Inside front cover illustrations courtesy of *American Antiques Graphic Society.*

Inside back cover illustrations (clockwise from top left) courtesy of *American Antiques Graphic Society, American Antiques Graphic Society, New York Public Library, New York Public Library.*

BROADWAY

A hardcover edition of this book was originally published in 1996 by Lyons & Burford, Publishers. It is here reprinted by arrangement with Lyons & Burford, Publishers.

Broadway Books titles may be purchased for business or promotional use or for special sales. For information, please write to: Special Markets Department, Bantam Doubleday Dell Publishing Group, Inc., 1540 Broadway, New York, NY 10036.

First Broadway Books trade paperback edition published 1997.

BROADWAY BOOKS and its logo, a letter B bisected on the diagonal, are trademarks of Broadway Books, a division of Bantam Doubleday Dell Publishing Group, Inc.

Designed by Catherine Lau Hunt

Library of Congress Cataloging-in-Publication Data

Jeffers, H. Paul (Harry Paul), 1934–
    The good cigar / H. Paul Jeffers and Kevin Gordon; with
illustrations by Kevin Gordon.
      p. cm.
    Includes bibliographical references and index.
    ISBN 0-7679-0036-7 (pb)
    1. Cigars. I. Gordon, Kevin. II. Title.
TS2260.J44 1997
679'.72—dc21   97-18998
                                            CIP

97 98 99 00 01 10 9 8 7 6 5 4 3 2 1

A good cigar is a smoke.

—*Rudyard Kipling*

CONTENTS

INTRODUCTION

"Have a Cigar!"

T his invitation is surely one of the happiest phrases in the
language.

Chances are your father celebrated your birth by handing
out cigars. NASA mission controllers invariably light up to mark the
success of a space venture. When astronaut John Glenn came back
from piloting America's historic first orbital Mercury flight he was
given the equivalent of his weight in Havana cigars. Notified of the rescue of a U.S. Air Force pilot who had been shot down in Bosnia,
President Clinton broke a rule banning smoking inside the White
House and lit a cigar. Great Britain's wartime Prime Minister, Winston
Churchill, held his cigar in the crook of fingers raised in a V as both
an instrument of defiance and an expression of confidence that he
soon would smoke it in salute to triumph. Following one devastating air
raid on London during the Nazi blitz, he immediately telephoned the
tobacco shop where he bought and stored his Havanas. "Don't be

concerned, sir," the proprietor assured him. "Your cigars are safe!" So was Britain.

As a remembrance of their meeting in Spain, Ernest Hemingway presented Ava Gardner with the band of his cigar. This romantic encounter took place following the bullfights, where victorious matadors were saluted with cries of "Olé!" and cigars all around.

A cigar became the indelible trademark of New York City's Mayor Fiorello La Guardia as he dashed to fires, smashed slot machines, and read comic strips to children on the radio during a newspaper strike. The tilt of a rakish cigar was as much the hallmark of Groucho Marx's comedy as were his low-slung walk, leer, and painted-on mustache. W.C. Fields brandished his omnipresent and half-smoked stogie as if it were a sword unsheathed against an enemy, whether it be the sheriff who had come to run him out of town, a nagging wife, or a nettlesome infant. "I haven't been sick a day since I was a child," said Fields. "A steady diet of cigars and whiskey cured me."

Like nothing else man-made, it is the virtue of the cigar that smoking one can be a powerful symbol, whether personal, social, political, or economic.

"Like all great art," wrote Thomas Simmons in the *New York Times,* "a cigar is iconoclastic. It wrecks all notions of civility and good behavior. A cigar announces revolution. At the same time it suggests the mystery of connoisseurship. Like all good mysteries, this one may arouse longing and even the envy the uninitiated feel toward the keepers of a strange, startling rite."

"By the cigars they smoke," said author John Galsworthy, "ye shall know the texture of men's souls."

Acceptance of cigar smoking has had its ups and downs since Galsworthy wrote those words.

Today, despite inroads made by the antismoking movement, cigars are suddenly fashionable. The "best of people" smoke, not sheepishly in the privacy of their homes, offices, and limousines, but proudly and in public. In addition to having a slick new magazine, *CIGAR Aficionado,* which first appeared in September 1992, available four times a year, cigarists seeking literary support can find it a dozen times annually in the pages of *The Cigar Monthly,* launched in 1993, and, since 1995, in the form of *Smoke Magazine.* This spritely periodical was the brainchild of Aaron L. Sigmund, and is published by a family that has been publishing on the subject of cigars since 1886 when Henry Lockwood introduced cigar retailers in New York to *Tobacco.* It was followed by *Smokeshop,* distributed to tobacco retailers in North America.

Yet long before these publications extolled the role of the cigar in the masculine world, a cigar maker and prophet of the sacred rite of smoking, Zino Davidoff, asked in *The Connoisseur's Book of the Cigar,* "What is there in a cigar that intensifies and prolongs the pleasure of smoking, which so attracts men? What is the noble quality the cigar brings to tobacco? How can one say that the cigar—nothing but an object—has a soul?"

The poet Lord Byron harbored no doubts. "Sublime Tobacco," he wrote. "Give me a cigar!"

Mark Twain smoked more than a score of cigars in a day and vowed that if cigar smoking were not allowed in Heaven he would gladly go to the other place.

In his memoir, *Summing Up,* Somerset Maugham confesses, "At the time when I was young and very poor, I only smoked cigars which were offered to me. I promised myself that if I ever had some money that I would savor a cigar each day after lunch and after dinner. This is the only resolution of my youth that I have kept, and the only realized ambition which has not brought dissolution."

In *The Gold Rush* Charlie Chaplin presents one of the most heart-tugging final scenes in the history of motion pictures as his "little tramp" retrieves the discarded and chewed stub of a millionaire's cigar and waddles away with it, puffing as happily as if he, too, were a rich man.

But cigar smoking is not just for the wealthy. Neither of the authors of this book is rich, although Kevin Gordon's introduction to cigar smoking was with a decidedly upscale Havana. In a positively Hemingwayesque moment he enjoyed his initial cigar (a Montecristo No. 3) in the Plaza de Toros in Madrid in 1982. As an aficionado and a novice matador he had actually ventured into the bullring twice and gotten himself fitted for a royal blue suit of lights. When not in Spain to run with the bulls in Pamplona or attending bullfights he celebrates unveilings of the portraits he paints for a living by lighting one of his favorite hand-rolled Havanas. Like many connoisseurs of Cuban tobacco, he longs for the day when travel to that island is permitted so he can obtain them legally.

Until then he generously shares with me the ones he manages to obtain while we engage in another mutual passion—or is it an obsession?—the pursuit of all there is to know about Sherlock Holmes in all his manifestations, from the original stories by Sir Arthur Conan Doyle to the television incarnation by the late Jeremy Brett. Although the mention of the Sleuth of Baker Street in a book about cigars may seem out of place, it is not. While the image of Sherlock is of a lean and hawkish figure enshrouded in a cloud of smoke as he puffs his way toward the solution of "a three pipe problem," Holmes is not only a cigar smoker but also an expert on them, their origins and makers, their tobaccos and their ashes. Cigars figure in several of his cases and lead to the solution of the mystery. In *The Sign of the Four,* the author of a monograph entitled "Upon the Distinction between the Ashes of the Various Tobaccos" explains to his associate and biographer, Dr. John H. Watson: "To the trained eye there is as much difference between the black ash of a Trichinopoly and the white fluff of the bird's-eye as there is between a cabbage and a potato."

In *The Boscombe Valley Mystery* Holmes deduces from a crime scene that includes the stump of a discarded cigar that the murderer is "a tall man, left-handed, limps with the right leg, wears thick-soled shooting-boots and a grey cloak, smokes Indian cigars, uses a cigar-holder, and carries a blunt penknife in his pocket." This last fact is discerned from the ragged manner in which the tip of the cigar has been cut; the absence of teeth marks make obvious the presence of the holder.

I employed no such amenity for my first venture into the world of cigars, on a dare when I was a college freshman in the 1950s in Philadelphia. My first was from a package of five-for-a-half-a-buck, machine-made, drugstore-bought Phillies. By the time I launched a career in broadcast journalism, I had graduated a bit upmarket to smoke Grenadiers. Although these six-in-a-pack-for-a-dollar cigars were hardly of the quality of the Havanas favored by sportscaster Howard Cosell after a steak at Manhattan's posh "21" restaurant, that did not dissuade him from bumming a Grenadier from me whenever our paths crossed in the 1960s at ABC News. But working in a newsroom never afforded one the atmosphere conducive to discovering whether cigars, indeed, have a soul.

For a period, cigars developed a bad reputation. The smoke-filled back room of shady politics, the cigar-chomping gangster, Clint Eastwood's ruthless gunman all cast cigars in an unflattering light.

Little wonder that the cigar's reputation suffered. Happily, though, this form of tobacco use has rebounded from its negative reputation to such an extent that the cigar is now a symbol of success in almost every aspect of American life as we near the end of the twentieth century. Cigar clubs and "cigar-friendly" restaurants have blossomed. Makers following the old tradition of the wine industry book the grand ballrooms of deluxe hotels for cigar "tastings." There's even a hit motion picture (*Smoke*) that seems destined to become a cult classic. A thoroughbred racehorse named Cigar thundered down the homestretches of the country's finest tracks. Celebrities and successful men and even a few women today boast of their affection for cigars.

Although some angry males may have turned to the cigar for its iconoclastic impact, most have discovered—as smokers have done through the centuries—that there is more to smoking a cigar than anyone who has never smoked one could ever appreciate.

In *The Good Cigar* you will find all aspects of the world of the cigar. From the most expensive to the least costly we offer everything there is to know about smoking them, whether you are already a connoisseur or still just a beginner. From the "discovery" of tobacco by European explorers to the process of making them; the history of cigar smoking in America; the cigar in literature and art; the romantic allure of the cigar store; the story behind the cigar store Indian, cigar bands, and boxes and those who smoked and smoke cigars—along with evaluations of brands and prices—we offer not only the "how-to" of cigars but also the *why*.

A Good Cigar

Oh, 'tis well and enough,

  A whiff or a puff

From the heart of a pipe to get;

And a dainty maid

Or a bubbling blade

May toy with the cigarette;

But a man, when the time

Of a glorious prime

Dawns forth like a morning star,

Wants the dark-brown bloom

And the sweet perfume

That go with a good cigar.

—NORRIS BULL

The Glorious Weed

From the bridge of his flagship *Santa Maria* on October 12, 1492, anchored in a gulf of what future maps would designate as San Salvador in the Bahamas, Christopher Columbus watched a man paddling a canoe heaped with dry leaves. Recording this observation in his journal, the explorer who had hoped to prove that by sailing westward from Spain he would find a quick, direct route to the riches of the Orient speculated that the man's cargo "must be a thing very much appreciated" by those who populated the islands.

Why this was so remained a mystery until a small group of Columbus's sailors went ashore at another island that the admiral described in his diary as being "as green as April in Andalusia." The singing of birds was such that it seemed as if one would not wish to depart. Flocks of garishly hued parrots obscured the sun. Beyond the blue sea's snowy breakers and the palm-fringed beaches stood lush trees of a thousand species. Behind them rose the sun-and-cloud-kissed sierra. The largest of the islands Columbus would claim for Spain he named Isla Juana in honor of the prince of Castile. Later it would be known as Fernandina. But native Taino Indians called it Colba, which Spanish tongues twisted into "Cuba."

When the landing party returned to report that this paradise that seemed to float between sea and sky was not China, Japan, or India, and that in this place there was no treasure to be found, they were able to provide Columbus with an answer to the riddle of the dried leaves. The men reported that the natives "perfume themselves with certain herbs" and "drank smoke." They also had a name for the curious dried leaves they set on fire in order to inhale the smoke—*cohiba* or *cojoba*.

Exactly where the name *tobacco* originated has been a matter of debate since the beginning of the influx of Europeans into the Western Hemisphere. It is known that the word *tabaco* was in use among the pre-Columbian natives of the West Indies. Some students of the origin of the term claim that it derives from the name of a state in Mexico (Tabasco) or from one of the Lesser Antilles (Tobago). An early explorer-priest, Bishop Bartolome de Las Casas, used the word *tabaco* in 1527 in reporting the smoking habits of Indians. The word also appeared in a treatise on the habits and customs of the peoples of the New World by sixteenth-century observer G.F. Oviedo y Valdes.

Wherever the name originated, over the next six centuries the brown leaves and the plant that produced them would prove to be far more valuable to the Spaniards and all those who followed them into Columbus's "New World" than gold or silver. Who among the inhabitants of the lands that Columbus opened to Old World exploration and exploitation were the first to cultivate and use the leaves of the tobacco plant is a question about which historians of the subject agree. Artifacts and picture writings show that the Mayans of the Yucatan region of Mexico incorporated smoking in their religious rituals. In one ceremony priests blew smoke to the four corners of the earth through a tube pipe. Medicine men drove out evil spirits with smoke and probably used clouds of fumes to conceal what they were doing.

What the religious class could not keep to themselves, however, was the tobacco plant itself. Because it was so widespread and readily available, the priests could not prevent the common folk from finding out the pleasurable effects of tobacco use in all its forms and harvesting it for themselves.

By the time Columbus and his ships arrived, tobacco growing and consumption had spread throughout the area these intruders presently named America. Although Columbus himself was not especially interested in smoking, his crew happily took up the practice and carried it home with them, as did the hordes of explorers and conquerors who came after them.

Pottery vessel found in Mexico and dated from the tenth century or earlier shows a Maya's string-tied cigar. Courtesy of New York Public Library

White invaders flooded in. Feverish with dreams of finding gold, Spaniards, Portuguese, English, and French collected islands, discovered continents, founded colonies, and sent home treasures of the New World that would have a profound influence on the lives of their homelands. Among the native products sent back were the potato, corn, and the dried leaves of the plant that could be rolled into a cylinder or put in a pipe and smoked to provide a unique sensation of taste and either exhilaration or relaxation.

Those who went back to Spain with tobacco also carried with them a name for what they were smoking. The Mayan verb *sikar,* meaning "to smoke," became the Spanish noun *cigarro.* That the cigar was the first form of tobacco to reach Europe was a matter of chance. As the tobacco historian Jerome E. Brooks points out in his book *The Mighty Leaf,* had the Spaniards first landed in North America above Mexico where locals chopped up the tobacco, stuffed it into small bowls, and inhaled the smoke through a long tube, they would have been pipe smokers, as were the English and French later. Had their first contact been with the Aztecs they would have smoked the

*Indian with "seegar" and man-size tobacco plant
(1738).* Courtesy of New York Public Library

reed-wrapped tubes of tobacco leaf that evolved into the paper-wrapped modern cigarette. But it was the cigar that these first voyagers carried back to Europe to share with family and friends. One propagandist for the practice of smoking proclaimed:

Let others praise the god of wine,
Or Venus, love and beauty's
smile;
I choose a theme not less divine,—
The plant that grows in
Cuba's isle.

The plant abounded in the lands encountered by Columbus and those who came after him because those regions provided the climatic conditions of warmth and wetness required for the tall, coarse, large-leafed perennial to flourish. Botanists classify it in the Nightshade family.

In full growth the tobacco plant stands as tall as a man. In producing seeds it is remarkably prolific. One scientist, Karl von Line, counted 40,320 in one pod, meaning a single plant had the potential to yield a million seeds.

That the dried leaves observed by Columbus and tasted by the most curious of his crewmen could be turned into a cash crop was not long in being realized. Carried home by the seafarers who shared their smokes with family and friends in the form of cigars or in pipes, tobacco became an instant sensation. Those who tried it wanted more; in the whole history of the world nothing had stirred the imagination of mankind quicker than the prospect of turning a personal profit by supplying someone else's demand.

Of course, there were those who observed in the pleasures of others the work of Satan. The precursors of the antismoking police who have persisted for more than half a millennium, they took to church pulpits to denounce it as "the Devil's revenge." The stuff was fit only for subhumans, they declared, such as the savages of the New World and slaves.

But some men of science noted that this import held within it the possibility of medicinal benefits. In 1560 the French ambassador to Portugal, Jean Nicot, wrote to the Grand Prior, Cardinal of Lorraine, that he had acquired an Indian herb that he applied to an ulcer, resulting in a cure. He observed that local herbalists were growing tobacco, pharmacists were stocking the leaves, and ordinary citizens were extolling

Nicotiana inserta infundibulo ex quo hauriunt fumū Indi & naucleri.

In "New Notebook of Plants" (1570), Pierre Pena and Matthias de l'Obel depicted the earliest printed illustration of the tobacco plant (Nicotiana tabacum). They also pictured a funnel-like object which natives of the "New World" called a "seegar." Spanish sailors turned the word into cigarillo. Courtesy of New York Public Library

the virtues of the plant as a healer. So impressed was Nicot that in a French-Latin dictionary that he published in 1573 he mentioned the medicinal virtues of this component of tobacco, to which he unabashedly assigned the name *Nicotiane*.

Later, after the tobacco plant had been studied and categorized as

a genus, the two main subspecies were also named for Nicot— *Nicotiana tabacum* and *Nicotiana rustica*.

While Nicot was compiling his dictionary, three other Frenchmen, Jean Liebault, Nicolas Monardes, and Gilles Everard, were at work separately in cataloging the therapeutic values of tobacco, including its uses as an unguent, powder, gargle, antiseptic, emetic, and cathartic in treating ailments from toothache to flatulence. Just what produced these effects was unknown until the mystery was solved by a French chemist, Louis Nicolas Vauquelin. He found an alkaloid component unique to tobacco that he called "Nicotinanine," after Nicot. The chemical is colorless, oily, and, in concentrated strength, a deadly poison. An internal dose of sixty milligrams is lethal to a healthy man. In an experiment by the Royal Society of England a single drop fed to a cat took one of the feline's nine lives in short order. Some students of Shakespeare's *Hamlet* suggest that the fatal potion administered to the melancholy Dane's father is a drop of nicotine. Many writers of modern mystery have also placed high concentrations of nicotine into the hands of murderers. Of course, nothing like the concentration of the chemical needed to kill has ever been found in the tobacco leaf itself. Although many cigars can be quite strong, they have never been so potent as to cause smokers to drop dead.

What neither Nicot's dictionary nor the writings of others on the subject of tobacco's medicinal powers mentions is the other aspect of tobacco use, one that did not pass unnoticed by the common folk—the sheer pleasure of smoking. It is this aspect of the plant, rather than its therapeutic potential, that ultimately fascinated the ordinary man and consequently stirred the interests of traders and merchants in satisfying the desire for tobacco—and turning a handsome profit.

Although experiments were conducted to see if tobacco might be grown at home, thereby saving the costs of transportation from the West Indies, the results were disappointing. Futhermore, why go through the process of growing, harvesting, curing the leaves, and manufacturing the end product when it was available in final form in the places where it grew naturally? A seemingly endless supply was available in Cuba, Trinidad, Venezuela, and other colonies to keep the people of Spain and Portugal satisfied, and to meet a growing appetite for tobacco in other countries.

Among non-Iberians who developed a liking for tobacco were the English, who had to pay a fancy price to import it from their archenemy, Spain. With the founding of English colonies on the North American mainland it was hoped that tobacco could be grown there. Among the adventurers who set sail in that hope was a swashbuckling poet named Walter Raleigh. In 1578, he and his brother Carew and half brother Sir Humphrey Gilbert outfitted a heavily armed fleet and took off on a "voyage of discovery." Unfortunately, storms and desertions aborted the effort. A decade later he tried again, and this time succeeded in founding a settlement on Roanoke Island in a colony he named for the "Virgin Queen." But the colony in Virginia not only failed, it also vanished, passing into history as "the lost colony" after Raleigh returned home.

Taking with him a supply of tobacco seeds, he hoped that by cultivating them in English soil he would free his countrymen of dependence upon the Spanish product. As in Roanoke, he failed. He was unable to persuade Englishmen to smoke the homegrown variety. Instead, self-styled "sophisticated" smokers in London liked the notion of smoking "Spanish." Despite its steep price, they preferred the imported tobacco, which they consumed in various ways. It was available in leaf form or coarsely spun into a thick twist about the size of a man's head, known as a "ball." "Cane" would be sweetened with rum, sugar, or molasses and rolled into a thin cigar. If compressed into a roll like a sausage and flavored with molasses it was a "pudding." Or it could be bought twisted like a rope, known as "cord," "pigtail," and "twist."

Ultimately, the cost of "Spanish" drove the English into a concerted effort to produce an acceptable English tobacco grown in the now thriving colony of Virginia. On arriving there in 1617 the new governor, Captain Samuel Argall, was informed by Captain John Smith that he would find that "the marketplace and streets and all other spare places [were] planted with tobacco."

That year the little colony exported 20,000 pounds of leaf to England, putting it on competitive footing with Spain and with a tobacco that was more suitable for the Englishman's preferred method of smoking—the pipe. Sir Walter Raleigh, who was knighted by Queen Elizabeth for accomplishments other than his championing of English tobacco, remained a stalwart pipe smoker—he lit up a pipe on the morning of his execution.

That unfortunate end to an adventurous life was ordered in 1681 by the successor to "Good Queen Bess," King James I, for whom history and the Protestant Church are indebted for the version of the Bible that bears his name. Those who enjoy the use of tobacco, however, view him as the worst foe of smoking of all time.

Raleigh's legacy, of course, was the establishment of tobacco as a commodity that could be cultivated successfully elsewhere in the Americas other than the tropical islands that were colonies of Spain. In the long run this incipient agriculture would develop into a vital segment of the art, craft, and business of cigar making in the United States.

However, before James ascended the throne and Raleigh laid his head on the executioner's chopping block at the Tower of London, tobacco had reigned supreme in "merrie olde England." The happy acceptance of smoking was noted in 1607:

Musicke, tobacco, sacke and sleep,
The tide of sorrow backward keep.

Legend, if not history, records that Raleigh even got Queen Elizabeth to try a pipe and that the monarch insisted that the Countess of Nottingham and all her maids "smoke out a whole pipe among them." A biographer of Raleigh wrote that tobacco "soon became of such vogue in Queen Elizabeth's court, that some of the great ladies, as well as the noblemen therein, would not scruple to take a pipe sometimes very sociably."

A German visitor to London in 1598 wrote home, "English are constantly smoking tobacco."

Then, like a sinister sovereign in a Shakespearean tragedy, into the saga of smoking there entered King James I. The son of Mary, Queen of Scots, he had been repulsed by smoking long before he put on a crown, first as James VI of Scotland in 1567,

Engraving in "lets voor allen" by Abraham van St. Clara, published in Amsterdam in 1745, illustrated stemming and twisting of tobacco into cigars. Courtesy of New York Public Library

then as James I of England in 1603. Within a year of his coronation his unremitting personal opposition to smoking was made official in a way that has always been a favorite of governments as a tool of oppression and suppression—taxation. In an attempt to discourage the importation of tobacco he raised the tariffs on the products of Virginia and Spain. The order to the High Treasurer of England hiking the tax by 4000 percent also provided the royal reasoning:

THE
GLORIOUS
WEED

9

Tabacco, being a drug of late years found out . . . is now at this day, through evil custom and the toleration thereof, excessively taken by a number of riotous and disordered persons of mean and base condition, who . . . do spend most of their time in that idle vanity.

That tobacco importation would be allowed at all is because James believed that it had been proved to be of some value medicinally. This consideration notwithstanding, he did all he could for more than a decade to harass the chief supplier of tobacco, the Virginia Company, in order to persuade Virginians to give up growing the plant. When asked why the colonists did not grow corn instead, Captain John Smith explained that the farmers sold the tobacco they raised at six times the price of corn.

But the King of England did not rely entirely on taxation to express his hatred of tobacco. In 1604 there appeared an antismoking tract entitled *A Counterblaste to Tobacco.* Although its authorship was not acknowledged, everyone knew it had been penned by James. Calling costly tobacco "precious stink," he accepted and repeated gossip that autopsies of smokers revealed "inward parts were soiled and infected with an oily kind of soot."

Perhaps hinting at the ultimate fate of Raleigh, whom James despised for many reasons other than Raleigh's championing of tobacco, James expressed astonishment that something "so vile and brought in by a father so generally hated, should be welcomed."

Smoking tobacco was, he continued, "a custom loathesome to the eye, hateful to the nose, harmful to the brain, dangerous to the lungs, and in the black stinking fume thereof, nearest resembling the horrible Stygian smoke in the pit that is bottomless."

Given the royal license to vent their wrath against smokers, others quickly authored similar works. One follower saw tobacco smoking as nothing less than "a plague, a mischief, a violent purger of goods,

Late 18th century tobacconists such as Carl Schnell sold tobacco in lavishly decorated paper bags. Courtesy of New York Public Library

Cigar bags of 19th century Netherlands provided protection for their contents and advertising for tobacco merchants. Courtesy of New York Public Library

lands, health, hellish, devilish, and damned tobacco, the ruin and overthrow of body and soul."

Tobias Venner unleashed a broadside with a title that may be the longest in the literature of tobacco—perhaps in all literature: "A Brief and Accurate Treatise concerning The taking of the Fume of Tobacco, Which very many, in these days doe too licentiously use. In which the immoderate, irregular, and unseasonable use thereof is reprehended, and the true nature and best manner of using it, perspicuously demonstrated."

Another scribe demonstrated a penchant for alliteration in warning smokers that tobacco was "very pernicious unto their bodies, too profluvious for many of their purses, and most pestiferous to the publike State."

Russian immigrants working in a cigar factory in Philadelphia, PA, at the turn of the century.
Courtesy of the Jacobs Collection

However, what proved to be most "pestiferous" to the state in the face of James's efforts at prohibition was an immediate increase in tobacco smuggling and the invention of clever ways to circumvent the law. For the Virginia Company the way to skirt the stiff taxes was to ship directly to Europe. Even though this was in contravention of the law it did not matter to Virginians. By that time tobacco had become king and Virginians, along with the citizens of the other English colonies in America, were developing a streak of independence that a century later would manifest itself in a decidedly rebellious manner.

Besides the burdens of taxation placed upon them by king and Parliament in England, tobacco growers in Virginia and Maryland, as well as in Kentucky, faced vigorous competition from tobacco-growing

Western Hemisphere colonies of other European powers. The French were exporting from Santo Domingo and Martinique and developing crops in Louisiana and even in Canada. Dutch planters in Curaçao were hard at work, as were the Portuguese in their colonies. Most important, Spain had established plantations in the West Indies, especially in Cuba's Vuelta Abajo district of the province of Pinar del Rio. At the western end of the island, its rich, tobacco-friendly soil favored a leaf of tantalizing aroma perfectly suited for rolling into cigars.

Contrary to the English, who had always favored the pipe, the smokers of Spain clung to their love of tobacco in the form brought home by Columbus's sailors. But as their appetite persisted there arose a desire for a more savory smoke than the harsh cigars that had been available from the dawn of smoking in Europe. To meet this demand for taste and aroma, Spanish botanists experimented with ways to improve the quality of tobacco for cigars. Manufacturers, primarily in Seville, tinkered and toyed with the techniques of producing them.

Late 19th century advertising "clip art" catalog offered illustrations for cigar merchants. Courtesy of New York Public Library

With the arrival of the high-quality, better-tasting leaf from Cuba, King Ferdinand VII issued a decree in 1821 encouraging the production of Cuban cigars by a state monopoly. The result was, in the phrase of tobacco historian Jerome E. Brooks, "the Age of the Cigar" in which the general spread of the cigar in Europe was expedited by the forced mingling of strangers in the Peninsular War of 1808–1814. "The British had conquered the French on Spanish soil," he wrote. "The cigar conquered them both."

British military campaigning had also been responsible for the introduction of the cigar in the English colonies of America. Accompanying the British army on an ultimately unsuccessful expedition to wrest Cuba from Spanish hands in 1762 was Colonel Israel Putnam. A Connecticut Yankee known as "Old Put"—who would become a general at the head of American troops fighting British redcoats in the American Revolution —he returned from Cuba with as many Havana cigars as the backs of three donkeys could carry.

Victorian era author Rudyard Kipling's poetry and prose extolled the virtues of the British Empire, warned Westerners not to try to "hustle the East" and penned the most famous phrase in the lore of the cigar—"A woman is only a woman, but a good cigar is a smoke." Courtesy of New York Public Library

Before long the farmers of Connecticut, who had been growing tobacco since they found Native Americans producing it in the earliest years of the colony, were attempting to grow the Cuban variety from seed for manufacturing into cigars in factories in Hartford. But try as they might, Connecticut-grown Cuban tobacco proved to be no rival to the real thing, although Connecticut-grown leaf turned out to be ideal

Cartoonist G. L. Stampa's 19th century drawing, "Humours of the Street," in which it is apparent that the British "Bobby" has decided to teach the boy a lesson about "the evils of tobacco" by destroying the kid's cigar. Courtesy of New York Public Library

as wrappers for such latter-day cigars as Macanudos and Davidoffs.

American cultivation of tobacco for cigars also flourished among Dutch settlers around Conestoga, Pennsylvania. A town that gave its name to the prairie schooners and freight wagons that traveled westward after the Civil War also gave birth to a term for cigars of all sizes and shapes, though the original "stogy" was thin and about a foot long.

According to the census of 1810, some 29 million cigars were manufactured in the United States, mostly in Pennsylvania. Production was also under way in Israel Putnam's Connecticut in the form of a "shoestring" variety used mainly for fillers of cheap cigars. But Connecticut

After waiting more than sixty years to succeed his anti-smoking mother, Victoria, as monarch of the British Empire, the Prince of Wales became King Edward VII and promptly greeted the tobacco-starved courtiers of Buckingham Palace with the happiest of phrases, "Gentlemen, you may smoke."

River Valley farmers also cultivated a leaf of fine texture and subtle odor called Maryland Broadleaf. New York manufacturers, employing immigrant labor that included children in "cigar factories" in the teeming tenements of the Lower East Side, turned out cheap, smelly cigars that were often available free in the city's multitudinous saloons as a lure to drinkers.

By 1880 the only states in the Union lacking a cigar factory were Montana and Idaho. But the chief source of cigars smoked in the United States in the nineteenth century was the West Indies, especially Cuba. A demand for the product in America and Europe in 1849 resulted in the tripling of the output of cigars in a variety of shapes and names. The best of these were Coronas, Imperials, Scepters, Kings, and Isabellas. Regalias were reserved for Spain's rulers; an especially thick Havana of far superior quality was made only for priests by monks.

Leaf exported from Cuba to factories in Philadelphia before the War of 1812 for manufacture of "Spanish" cigars was used as wrapper. The filler was likely to be Kentucky-grown. Factory-made products, they were sold as "long nines," "short sixes," and "supers" and usually cost $16 a thousand.

Names for such cigars were less regal than those from Cuba. Americans smoked Wedding Cake, People's Choice, Cherry Ripe, Henry Clay, Daniel Webster, and a host of others with distinctly democratic names. The explosion of manufacturing reflected a generally intensified demand for manufactured products of all kinds. This phenomenon also created a consumer demand for quality. During the years before the Civil War every cigar smoker knew the differences between "stogy" and "Spanish," or "Havana."

Although the cigar had attained a great deal of popularity in the first half of the nineteenth century, the Civil War ushered in what might be called the Golden Age of the Cigar in the United States. Not to be underestimated in the increased popularity of cigars was that some very important personages smoked them, including the two generals who had won the war, Ulysses S. Grant and William Tecumseh Sherman. Nor did the cigar suffer from its association with Mark Twain.

In an 1883 essay, "Smoking as Inspiration," the creator of Tom Sawyer and Huckleberry Finn proudly claims that he began smoking "immoderately" when he was eight years old "with one hundred cigars a month." By the time he was twenty he had increased his allowance to two hundred a month and before he was thirty to three hundred a month. But he did point out that he would "only smoke one cigar at a time."

Twain and other men of distinction gave encouragement to smokers and appeared to give the lie to a nasty quip by newspaper publisher Horace Greeley that a cigar "is a fire at one end and a fool at the other."

Should a late-nineteenth-century American cigar smoker care to look elsewhere for validation he could turn to Rudyard Kipling. In his poem *The Betrothed* the British author muses at length on a "quarrel about Havanas" between a man and his wife, Maggie, who has challenged him to "choose between me and your cigar."

With "Open the old cigar-box, get me a Cuban stout," the man and the poem deliberate the options before asking of the cigars, "Who is Maggie that I should abandon you?" It ends:

A million surplus Maggies are willing to bear the yoke;
And a woman is only a woman, but a good cigar is a smoke.
Light me another Cuba: I hold to my first-sworn vows,
If Maggie will have no rival, I'll have no Maggie for a spouse.

As a representative of the decade of the 1890s—known in Great Britain as the Victorian era and in America as the Gilded Age and the Gay Nineties—Kipling was perhaps second in fame only to the monarch who lent her name to those years. But like her sixteenth-century predecessor on the English throne, James I, Queen Victoria was no friend to smoking. Although the British Isles were suffused with the smoke of cigars and pipes, Buckingham Palace and other royal domiciles were not. Smoking around Victoria Regina was banned even for her son and heir, the Prince of Wales. Should "Bertie," as he was known to the aristocrats, artists, and other personalities of London, including the circle that formed around witty Oscar Wilde, wish to smoke he had to light up elsewhere. Consequently, after waiting until he was in his sixties to don the crown as Edward VII, it is not surprising that he immediately turned to the men of his court and announced firmly, "Gentlemen, you may smoke."

The king and his welcome change in smoking policy would be immortalized in a brand of cigar, the King Edward. Had she been around, it is safe to assume that Victoria would not have been at all amused. Nor would she have been keen on the naming of a brand of American pipe tobacco after her beloved consort, Prince Albert.

By the year of Victoria's Diamond Jubilee (1898) the annual consumption of cigars in the United States had surpassed 4 billion. In 1920 the number sold had reached 7 billion. So great was the demand for tobacco in all its forms that in 1913 domestic output totaled 266,678 tons. According to one writer, "The weight of the tobacco consumed in the United States in a year is equal to the weight of the entire and combined populations of Delaware, Maryland, Virginia, West Virginia,

North and South Carolina, Georgia, Florida, Tennessee, Alabama, and the District of Columbia."

Cigars were now available in all shapes, sizes, blends, and prices, from those of small makers who sold only regionally to those of large manufacturers with national distribution backed by extensive advertising and merchandising campaigns. Everyone who wished to smoke, no matter his financial means, could find a cigar of agreeable flavor at a reasonable price.

Despite the abundance of choices, there remained room for complaint. And in the category of gripers no one has ever equaled Vice President of the United States Thomas Marshall (1914–1921). Carrying out his constitutional duties by presiding over the U.S. Senate, he listened to one senator reciting a list of things the senator thought the country needed. In a stage whisper loud enough to be heard and recorded for posterity, Marshall declared, "What this country needs is a good five-cent cigar."

But what, exactly, did he mean?

What *is* a good cigar?

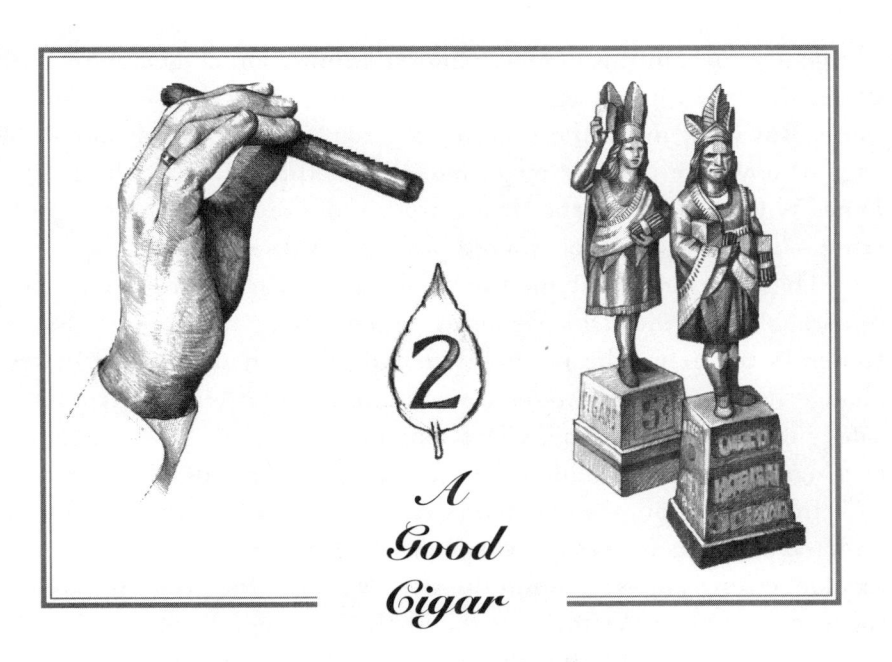

2
A Good Cigar

A WELL-CHOSEN CIGAR IS LIKE ARMOR AND IS
USEFUL AGAINST THE TORMENTS OF LIFE.
—*Zino Davidoff*

O n a glorious evening in May 1992 that only the climate of
southern California could produce, a string quartet took up
instruments and filled a hall of the sumptuous Ritz-Carlton
hotel in seaside Laguna Niguel with the music of Bach. A banquet
table offered the delights of lobster rivoli, rare filet mignon, ripe
cheeses, and champagne. Gathered to luxuriate in the surroundings,
food, and music were corporate executives, politicians, celebrities from
the world of entertainment, and Marine generals—in all, 157 men in
black tie and three elegantly dressed women.

At first glance the occasion appeared to be another gala on behalf of a good cause, in this case a memorial foundation dedicated to Ruth Berle, the late wife of legendary comedian ("Mr. Television") Milton Berle. But what made the evening different enough to warrant a full page of coverage in *Time* magazine is what the author of the article, James Willwerth, called the "true purpose" of those at the glittery gathering—"to indulge in their shared passion." A good cigar.

That an event glorifying the smoking of cigars took place at all is remarkable. As the *Time* reporter noted, since the 1964 Surgeon General's report on the perils of smoking there had followed "a seachange in American attitudes toward tobacco that eventually pushed sales into a steady decline. Cigar fans faced not only dirty glares but also signs and waiters telling them to butt out of public places."

Indeed, the Surgeon General's report had loosed a flood of enmity directed against smokers the vitriol of which had not been seen in history since King James's "counterblaste." Not even the dour dismissal of tobacco by Queen Victoria matched the vehemence of the "smoke police" of the United States during the last third of the twentieth century. At times it seemed the slogan "Thank you for not smoking" and other emblems of the antitobacco crusade were in bloom everywhere, even in the heart of the tobacco-growing states. Taking a leaf (no pun intended) from King James, the no-smoking militants enlisted the power of government in the cause, succeeding in banning tobacco advertising from radio and television and seeking its prohibition in all the media of mass communication (the First Amendment notwithstanding), and through the stultifying effects of taxation.

Yet, as *Time*'s reporter in Laguna Niguel wrote, "Sealed from the hotel lobby and society's opprobrium, these 'lovers of the leaf' were happily turning the air blue with the smoke from their premium cigars."

How and why had this happened?

Willwerth ventured the opinion that the premium cigar had staged a stunning "clandestine comeback" because of a "demographic phenomenon that has helped so many other luxury products: the emerging class of wealthy baby boomers who have apparently concluded that fine cigars complement the country house and the wine collection. And as luxuries go, even the classiest cigars are a lot more affordable than, say, a new BMW. In addition to the boomers is a core of veteran smokers who simply like the rich experience a good cigar provides them."

Statistics bore out the reasoning. Consumption of the high-priced brands was at double the levels of fifteen years earlier. Sales of cigars costing $1.25 or more had leapt from 50 million in 1974 to 100 million. Among the upscale purchasers were millionaires (accounting for 38 percent of sales) and a far greater number of buyers whose incomes afforded them at least two cars and such amenities as antiques, status-symbol wristwatches costing more than $500, and frequent and expensive travels abroad. According to a survey of readers of *CIGAR Aficionado,* the average weekly expenditure for premium cigars was about $26.

In brief, in the view of the magazine's founder and editor, Marvin Shanken, in an interview in the *New York Times* on September 8, 1993, such a smoker was someone confident in his lifestyle. "An overachiever. Someone who is maybe even a part-outlaw in spirit."

Among the celebrants, if not outlaws, at the Laguna Niguel event in 1992 were Henry R. Schielein, Vice President and General Manager of the host hotel and himself a cigar connoisseur, and Richard DiMeola, Executive Vice President, Consolidated Cigar Corporation, and head of its premium cigar subsidiary, Tabacalera de Garcia in the Dominican Republic. Over two days of the "cigar event" the two engaged in a dialogue on the subject of how to judge whether a cigar is "good."

The essence of their discussion and their conclusions were published in question-and-answer format in a small pamphlet, "How to Judge a Good Cigar." Because this condensation of their talk provides an illuminating and helpful guide to some of the most basic tenets of cigar choice, the results are further digested here as a foundation for all that will follow in this book's exploration of the world of the cigar.

Q: WHAT IS THE SINGLE MOST IMPORTANT FACTOR IN DETERMINING THE QUALITY OF A FINE, ALL-NATURAL TOBACCO, LONG-FILLED, HANDMADE CIGAR?
A: *Consistency of quality in tobacco and construction.*

Q: CAN QUALITY BE JUDGED BY TESTING ONLY ONE CIGAR?
A: *The greater the number evaluated, the greater the accuracy.*

Q: WHAT MAKES A CIGAR'S CONSTRUCTION IMPORTANT?
A: *If a cigar is made by skimping on the number of leaves in the filler, it will draw too easily and produce burning and harshness. If overfilled, it will be hard, if not impossible, to draw, thereby providing a much lower volume of smoke, taste, and aroma—all of which are the chief pleasures of cigar smoking.*

Q: WHAT OTHER CHARACTERISTICS OF CONSTRUCTION SHOULD BE CONSIDERED?
A: *The aesthetics. The cigar should look good and feel good to the touch. It should have life in it.*

Q: HOW IMPORTANT IS THE TOBACCO?
A: *Not only must the tobacco be of consistent high quality, but it also must be correctly processed.*

Q: ARE WHEN AND WHERE A CIGAR IS SMOKED IMPORTANT?
A: *A cigar will taste different depending upon when it's smoked: morning or evening, after a meal, with coffee or cognac, indoors or outdoors.*

Q: IS THE PRICE INDICATIVE OF QUALITY OR CONSISTENCY?
A: *High prices do not guarantee a good cigar.*

"As a rule, with cigars as with food and wine," advise Schielein and DiMeola, "if you like the taste and aroma it's good. And, if that pleasing taste and aroma is delivered every time, the cigar is 'good.'"

A quarter of a century before cigar lovers gathered in the posh Ritz-Carlton in Laguna Niguel, a man with a reputation as a modern arbiter of the good cigar, Zino Davidoff, wrote in *The Connoisseur's Book of the Cigar,* "It is made for all the senses, for all the pleasures, for the nose, the palate, the fingers, the eyes. . . . A good cigar contains the promise of a totally pleasurable experience. . . . To know how to smoke is to recover certain forgotten rhythms, to re-establish communication with the self. If there is a secret of the cigar, it is to be found in the slow movements, the dignified, measured smoking. The movements are more than mannerisms; they are ceremonial acts."

Davidoff's advice continues:

> **When you examine a well-chosen cigar, hold it between the index finger and the thumb. The subtle pleasure it offers may be anticipated by inspecting the color of the wrapper, the shape of the cigar, its length, by feeling its solidness, and by smelling its aroma.**

This is sound advice, as well, for the cigar lover whose economic status forbids shelling out $26 a week for the top-of-the-line cigars preferred by subscribers to Shanken's magazine. Standards applied to the choice of an expensive handmade corona smuggled into the United States in defiance of the embargo on Cuban cigars should also be employed to judge whether a machine-made domestic variety, bought five in a pack from the newsstand or drugstore, is worth the price—a "good" cigar.

How Cigars Are Made

No matter where they are bought or the price paid for them, the process of making a cigar begins with the cultivation of the tobacco. It is intensive, tedious, largely done by hand, and comparable in many ways to the making of wine. Just as the pedigree of the grape is basic to winemaking, the quality of the tobacco leaves used for making cigars is crucial.

Of the two species, N. *tabacum* is the chief one for commercial use in North America, while N. *rustica* is harvested for local consumption in the Far East. The taller of the species, N. *tabacum* produces broad green leaves with long, soft hairs that exude moisture that is glutinous to the touch. Although of varying shapes and sizes, the leaves are usually oblong with pointed tips and are attached to a cylindrical stalk. Its flower, if allowed to bloom, is light rose in color. As noted earlier, the seeds are small and abundant.

In commercial cultivation they are planted in flat fields and then carefully shaded from the sunlight with cloth or straw. Sprouting takes place in five to eight days. As growth proceeds the covers are gradually removed. When sufficiently matured they are transplanted to grow naturally in larger fields until they have reached the point of harvest, usually in a month. At that point the initial dull green leaves appear lighter and more brilliant. When the plants reach the budding stage, the buds are removed to prevent stunting. At harvesting comes the meticulous hand-picking of the leaves and the sorting of them for particular uses in the cigar. Should a light (*claro*) cigar be desired the leaf will be cut prematurely. If the leaf is left to maturity it is assessed as to size (large, average, small) and condition. A good leaf suitable for wrapper may be sufficient for about thirty cigars.

The location of leaves on the plant is a factor in how they will be used. Physical relation to the plant determines the form, whether in cigarettes, pipes, or as wrapper or filler in cigars, both inexpensive and premium. The finest, found in the middle of the plant, go for wrappers. Those from the top and bottom, judged for their bulk and burning qualities, are blended for filler, depending on flavor desired—mild, medium, full.

Each of the three parts of a cigar makes a contribution. The wrapper's is visual and aesthetic. Its color presents a guide to flavor: the darker the hue, the stronger. It must not be too oily, and should have a subtle bouquet. And its veins must not protrude. Delicately squeezed between the thumb and forefinger, the wrapper should be soft and pliable. It is the most costly ingredient of the cigar.

Immediately within the wrapper is the binder leaf. Usually, this consists of two halves of the coarse leaf from the upper part of the plant. Its virtue is its good tensile strength, needed to contain the filler.

Made of separate leaves, the filler forms the "insides" of the cigar and is rolled to permit easy draw of the smoke. Blending of leaves for filler dictates size and flavor.

As judging and sorting continue, the leaves are bundled and taken to be cured in barns in which both temperature and humidity are carefully regulated. Tied to poles and hung in a manner to ensure good air circulation, the leaves dry over a period of forty-five to sixty days, during which they turn from green to a golden brown. At the end of the drying procedure they are taken down, examined again for quality, and bundled according to grade, size, and color. In the next phase they are stripped of midribs and culled of broken leaves, then stored for another thirty-five to forty days for fermentation.

In this process the leaves lie in huge "bulks" during which their centers generate heat. To ensure uniform heating, the leaves are manipulated. In a process known as "sweats" the bulks are turned between four and eight times. If this were not done the leaves would become overly fermented, or "spent," and lose flavor and aroma.

The result of fermentation is purging of the high levels of the tar, acidity, and nicotine found in cigarettes, leaving the cigar tobacco more mellow and palatable—and healthier. The leaves are then gathered in small bundles called "hands" and eventually put into casks to age further, sometimes for years.

When deemed ready to be made into cigars they are delivered to manufacturers. Whether it is performed by individuals who are skilled in the art of hand wrapping or by machinery of assembly-line factories, this part of the process—like all that has happened before—is a major component in turning a "weed" into an object of pleasure.

As Jerome E. Brooks noted in *The Mighty Leaf*, "Tobacco may seem a rough, rank weed to some, but its nature is fragile and it demands a kind of brooding care."

The poet Henry James Mellen put it this way:

> *Weed of the strange flower, weed of the earth,*
> *Killer of dullness, parent of mirth,*
> *Come in the sad hour, come in the gay,*
> *Appear in the night, or in the day,—*
> *Still thou art as welcome as June's blooming rose,*
> *Joy of the palate, delight of the nose.*
> *Weed of the green field, weed of the wild,*
> *Fostered in freedom, America's child,*
> *Come in Virginia, come in Havana,*
> *Friend of the universe, sweeter than manna.*

Another poet (anonymous, alas) chose a non-Biblical metaphor for tobacco, comparing it to the legendary lotus of classical literature and mankind's vain quest to find it:

> *The Old World wearied of the long pursuit.*
> *And called the sacred leaf a poet's theme,*
> *When lo! the New World, rich in flower and fruit,*
> *Revealed the lotus, lovelier than the dream*
> *That races of the long past did haunt,—*
> *The green-leaved, amber-tipped tobacco plant.*

Now transformed from "weed" to "cured," the "lotus" leaves arrive at the most crucial stage of their journey from field to cigar. What sort of cigars they will be depends upon how they are made, whether mass-produced in a factory or rolled one at a time at the bench of a skilled artisan.

The best tobacco, the most careful processing, and the right blending mean nothing if the cigar is not properly constructed. If it is underfilled or made by skimping on the number of leaves in the filler it is likely to have air pockets that will cause a fast burn and a hot smoke. If it is overfilled it might prove to be "plugged" and therefore impossible to draw. Uneven burning is invariably a sign of an improper roll. The right filling will result in a cigar that burns evenly and produces ash that is relatively firm. Consistently loose and flaky ash marks a poorly constructed cigar. A cigar that has been made correctly should feel firm and resilient in the hand and have good mouth feel. Soft and squishy is a sure sign of poor construction.

Whether a cigar is made by hand or by machine, the process is dictated by the anatomy of the cigar. Either way, a cigar consists of filler, binder, and wrapper. The essential difference between the handmade and one turned out by a machine is in the makeup of the filler. That of the hand-rolled cigar is just that—hand rolled. Two to four filler leaves of the length of the type of cigar being made are placed end to end and then rolled into the two halves of the binder leaves. This is called the "bunch" and forms the bulk of the single cigar that will be completed by encasing with wrapper leaf and trimming.

In machine-made cigars the combination of filler leaves and binder is achieved in a manner similar to the one used to make cigarettes. The blended filler is fed through a mechanism that compresses it into a long, continuous rod. Covered by a sheet of binding leaf, the rod is then automatically cut for length, fitted with a rounded end called a "cap," and sealed. The wrapper is applied by another machine. Trimmed again, the cigars are individually wrapped in cellophane (the cigar band is often imprinted on it) and put in boxes for retail sale, either singly or in pocket-sized cardboard packages containing three to six cigars.

While the handmade cigar is produced in much the same way, the difference between a hand-rolled and a machine-made cigar has been compared to the difference between possessing a copy of a masterpiece painting and owning the original.

Like an artist, the person who manufactures cigars by hand finds satisfaction in the process as well as in the completed product. In a promotional brochure put out by makers of Macanudo cigars, an employee compares the thrill of unbaling a shipment of wrapper leaves that have been aged almost three years to "opening a precious gift." Baled eight rows across, the leaves were grown and processed in the state where Israel "Old Put" Putnam had planted his Cuban tobacco seeds in 1762 in hopes of placing Connecticut in the first rank of tobacco growing in the colonies. Two and a half centuries later that dream had become a reality.

Called "the perfect place to make a good cigar" in an August 13, 1995, article in the *New York Times,* Connecticut was lauded for producing tobacco that was termed "the platinum of the cigar-making world." Called "Connecticut Shade," or just "Shade," it has achieved premium status because the superb qualities found in its "golden brown, unblemished" leaves are ideal as wrapper for some of the world's finest cigars. Grown in carefully shaded fields in the Connecticut River Valley and benefiting from its cigar-friendly soil, they are shipped to the Dominican Republic for a year of curing, then sent back to Connecticut for fermentation (a two-year process), and finally taken to Jamaica to be hand-rolled into the Macanudo cigars of General Cigar Company.

Once the "precious gift" of Connecticut Shade has been received and uncrated, the leaves are sorted and graded according to length, cleanliness, and color from light yellow-gold to deep brown. Marred leaves are discarded and the remainder stripped of stems, inspected, and divided into hands to begin the fermentation process.

Upon completion of the aging process, the blending begins. In this instance what is sought is a combination of Jamaican, Dominican, and Mexican filler leaves, which are placed in cedar boxes and cedar storage rooms for three weeks to allow the aromas of the different leaves to "marry." A buncher then takes the leaves and rolls them with fingers inside a dark, supple Mexican binder.

The next step is to place the bunch into a wooden mold that fits the length with a gauge called a "ring." This is a measure of the diameter of the cigar in increments of $1/64$ inch. Thus, a cigar an inch thick has a ring gauge of 64. However, ring gauge need not be proportional to length. The Gran Corona/Montecristo A is $9^1/_4$ inches long with a ring gauge of 47, while a Churchill has the same ring gauge but is 7 inches in length. A $4^1/_2$-inch Panatela has a ring gauge of 26 and the same-length Tres Petit Corona a 40. Although the girth of a cigar relates to flavor (the thicker it is, the fuller the flavor), neither ring gauge nor length has anything to do with the quality of the cigar. In measuring whether a cigar is "good" it is the quality of the leaf that matters, along with the manner of manufacture. If price is not a concern, it is reasonable to expect that handmade cigars will be more satisfying than machine-made. Of course, as with any product the consumer may reasonably anticipate that an object that has been made by hand, presumably with tender, loving care, will always be the better buy.

Making cigars by hand is not an occupation that can be mastered quickly; those engaged in it have gone through a long apprenticeship and expect the work to last a lifetime. As in any intensely personal occupation, these craftspeople tend to become specialists in some aspect of the work. In the world of the handmade cigar these specialties are bunchers, wrapper-rollers, trimmers, inspectors, selectors, and those who put on the paper bands and either wrap the cigars in cellophane and put them in glass tubes, or leave them unwrapped before packing them in boxes.

In the making of prized Cuban cigars there are more than two hundred stages in the manufacturing process, from seeding to shipping. Rollers (*torcedores*) are responsible for shepherding a cigar from

A woman "taster" in the Philippines. Courtesy of New York Public Library

bunching to trimming for size. Working at a bench (*la tabla*) with a flat, rounded knife (a *chavete*), the accomplished roller can finish about one hundred medium-sized cigars per eight-hour day, six days a week. The average output is about fifty-six. In addition to their salary, workers may be rewarded by being permitted to take home five cigars a day and to smoke as many as they wish at work. To help break the monotony of such a repetitive job, an employee with an especially pleasing voice is likely to be designated *lector de tabaceria*. The job entails reading to the others, although this form of mental diversion often has been replaced by the playing of a radio.

In a cigar factory, job status is important. The most skilled workers sit at the front of the room (*galera*) and the less accomplished at the rear.

Perhaps, at first thought, the best job in cigar making is that of taster. These professional smokers (*catadores*) check on aroma, draw, and other crucial aspects of quality control. To do so they do not smoke an entire cigar, of course—only about an inch of it. To freshen the palate they sip sugarless tea. And the tasting is done only in the morning.

The output is also judged for wrapper color. The darker the hue, the stronger the smoke. From lightest to darkest they are:

Category	Color, strength/taste, aroma
Double claro	greenish brown, very mild; also called Candela or Claro claro
Claro (also called Natural)	pale brown, mild
EMS (English Market Selection)	Designation for the shade of wrapper preferred in the British cigar market: slightly deeper in tone than claro
Colorado claro	midbrown, well matured
Colorado	reddish dark brown, aromatic
Colorado maduro	dark brown, less aromatic
Maduro	very dark, for a seasoned smoker
Oscuro	black, strong with little aroma

All of these colors are found in all sizes and shapes of cigars. These are categorized by style, which is determined by the style of the head (the

Style	Inches/ ring	Body	Foot
Giant	over 8; 46 or more	straight	open
Double Corona	$6^3/4$–$7^1/8$; 49–54	straight	open
Churchill	$6^3/4$–$7^1/8$; 46–48	straight	open
Belicoso	$5^1/2$; 52	straight	open
Pyramid/ Torpedo	$4^3/4$–7; 50–60	tapered	open
Toro	$5^5/8$–$6^5/8$; 48–54	straight	open
Robusto	4–$5^1/2$; 48–54	straight	open
Grand Corona	$5^5/8$–$6^5/8$; 45–57	straight	open
Corona Extra	5–$5^1/2$; 45–57	straight	open
Giant Corona	more than $7^1/4$; 40–45	straight	open
Lonsdale	$6^1/2$–$7^1/4$; 40–45	straight	open

Style	Inches/ ring	Body	Foot
Long Corona	$5^7/8$–$6^3/8$; 40–44	straight	open
Corona	$5^1/4$–$5^3/4$; 40–44	straight	open
Petit Corona	4–$5^1/8$; 40–44	straight	open
Culebra	$5^3/4$; 39	flat, braided	open
Long Panatela	7 or more; 35–39	straight	open
Panatela	$5^1/2$–$6^7/8$; 35–39	straight	open
Short Panatela	$4^5/8$; 35–39	straight	open
Especial	$7^1/2$; 38	straight	open
Slim Panatela	5 and more; 30–34	straight	open
Small Panatela	4–5; 30–34	straight	open
Demi-Tasse	4; 30	straight	open
Cigarillo	under 4; under 29	straight	open

As Nat Sherman posed outside his Manhattan store he claimed that his cigar was the world's longest. At fourteen inches long, it probably was not, but it made a great publicity photo. Courtesy of Nat Sherman

part that goes in the mouth), length, thickness (ring gauge), shape of the body, and the foot (the end that is lighted). See chart on previous page.

The longest cigar is the Cuba Aliados General at 18 inches with a ring gauge of 66. In *The Connoisseur's Book of the Cigar* Zino Davidoff categorizes the Corona as "the king of the cigars," embodying everything that is necessary to satisfy the veteran smoker, whereas the larger "double corona," often compared to a chair rung, is associated with "those men who are searching for a special effect" or those who would feel comfortable seated at the gambling table or in a nightclub, a magnum of champagne within easy reach. On the other hand, the Lonsdale is "an imperious cigar" marvelously adapted to magnificent dinners and elegant evenings.

In enjoying a cigar no factor is more important than when it is smoked. Davidoff wrote, "Don't forget, a cigar is a companion, and a rare one that will never slip away. You can call upon it at any time. But different cigars suit different circumstances or situations." Hotelier Henry Schielein and cigar company executive Richard DiMeola, in "How to Judge a Good Cigar," note that a cigar will have a different taste depending upon whether it is morning or evening. Most veteran cigar smokers contend that the time of day dictates the choice of cigar. Their recommendation for between breakfast and lunch is small and mild. Their choice for immediately after lunch is one that complements what has been eaten. Light meal? A light cigar. Medium-weight gastronomy: medium-weight cigar. Afternoon smoking calls for cigars that are light, short, and not too strong. Regarding "the postprandial" smoke of the evening, the choice should be made on the same basis by which a general decides on strategy and tactics in planning a battle. The decision depends on "the situation and the terrain."

The Welsh poet Dylan Thomas's *A Child's Christmas in Wales* paints a word picture of Yuletide after-dinners: "Some few large men sat in the front parlors without their collars, uncles almost certainly, trying their new cigars, holding them out judiciously at arms' length, returning them to their mouths, coughing, then holding them out again as though waiting an explosion."

For nineteenth-century America's most celebrated author, Mark Twain, an evening of after-dinner cigar smoking with twelve friends at his home provided an opportunity to get even with associates who constantly accused him of preferring "the worst cigars in the world." How he visited retribution on them and proved "what superstition, assisted by a man's reputation, can do," he describes in his 1890 essay "Concerning Tobacco."

Samuel Langhorne Clemens, better known as Mark Twain, gave the world Tom Sawyer and Huckleberry Finn, and let it be known that if cigar smoking were not permitted in Heaven, he would happily go to the other place. Courtesy of New York Public Library

"One of them was as notorious for costly and elegant cigars as I was for cheap and devilish ones," he wrote. "I called at his house and when no one was looking borrowed a double handful of his very choicest; cigars which cost him forty cents apiece and bore red-and-gold labels in sign for their nobility. I removed the labels and put the cigars into a box with my favorite brand on it—and brand which all these people knew, and which cowed them as men are cowed by an epidemic. They took these cigars when offered and sternly struggled with them—in dreary silence, for hilarity died when the fell brand came into view and started around—but their fortitude held for a short time only; then they made excuses and filed out, treading on one another's heels with indecent eagerness; and in the morning when I went out to observe results the cigars lay all between the front door and the gate. All except one—that one lay in the plate of the man from whom I had cabbaged the lot. One or two whiffs was all he could stand. He told me afterward that some day I would get shot for giving people that kind of cigars to smoke."

Another nineteenth-century cigar smoker, Robert T. Lewis, saw in the after-dinner cigar a panacea for all that happened during the day. If events were difficult, pleasant, lyrical, or savage, and regardless of whether one fought, loved, or suffered, the smoking of a cigar presented an opportunity to contemplate on what it all meant.

He wrote, "The blue smoke of a well-chosen cigar disappears into the air, a symbol, perhaps, of the vanity and precariousness of all things. No other object or person is capable of giving such an opportunity to indulge in introspection and to contemplate one's own being."

The poet Henry S. Leigh agreed:

> *When Fear and Care and grim Despair*
> *Flock round me in a ghostly crowd,*
> *One charm dispels them all in air,—*
> *I blow my after-dinner cloud.*

The English writer C.S. Calverly penned:

> *Sweet when the morn is gray;*

Sweet when they've cleared away
Lunch; and at close of day
Possibly sweetest!

Regarding when *not* to take out a cigar and light it up, one wit advised against smoking if hunting bear, wolf, or boar. The Mexican bandit Pancho Villa ordered his gang not to smoke cigars before a raid, lest the pungent smell of smoke alert the intended targets to their depredations. The readers of the adventures of Sherlock Holmes have learned that the criminal had better not smoke a cigar at the scene of the crime.

Lighting a cigar (or anything else) is clearly not a good idea when at a gasoline station filling up your car's tank. If aviation is a passion, the same rule must be applied when the airplane is being fueled. Other venues where a lighted cigar is discouraged or forbidden by fire laws include hospital rooms and other places in which oxygen tanks are present, theater auditoriums, and other crowded areas presenting the danger of fire.

Not lighting a cigar is also in order if confronted by a NO SMOKING sign (in any language), in churches and synagogues, if traveling in most Islamic countries, and at any place where the authorities have banned smoking. Obviously, no respectable citizen may go against the law.

Smoking is also ill advised when the person closest to you fixes you with an icy stare to convey the message that "if you light that thing in my presence you will suffer serious physical injury." Of course, no gentleman or lady would smoke in a place where it is not welcome, although whether to enter such a situation in the first place is a legitimate question.

Unfortunately, the number of individuals expressing opposition to smoking has increased enormously since the 1964 Surgeon General's report on smoking and health triggered the "no-smoking movement," resulting in what many smokers perceive as the smoke police. The result has been an increase in the number of places that have banned cigar smoking, either as a result of the passage of restrictive laws or because of the efforts of highly organized and strenuously vocal anti-smoking pressure groups.

Ironically and sadly, all of this transpired despite the fact that cigars have never been deemed dangerous to the health of the smoker or those exposed to cigar smoke. Unfortunately, this negative public perception of cigars had more than social implications and consequences. It also precipitated a reaction by government in the form of punitive legislation trying to force a change in private behavior through the age-old—and odious—device of taxation. In spite of an assertion by President Ronald Reagan in his inaugural address of January 20, 1981, that taxing power "must not be used to regulate the economy or bring about social change," a study by the Cigar Association showed that before 1980 only seven states had imposed taxes on cigars. Since then that number had increased to thirty-five, with Oregon, Utah, Minnesota, and Hawaii imposing a cigar tax of 35 percent or more and Washington a staggering 64.9 percent. Adding to the levy on cigars were numerous cities and counties.

These social and economic pressures provoked a precipitous decline in the cigar industry, especially in the United States, where the antismoking forces were at their most virulent. From a high of nearly 9 billion in 1964, sales of all premium cigars declined in the United States to 2 billion in 1992. Over three decades the annual rate of sales maintained a steady 4 to 5 percent decline. While 101 million premium cigars were imported in 1981, only 99 million were imported in 1992. And in the second half of 1994 buyers of premium cigars discovered that many brands were out of stock because of diminished demand.

Especially hard hit by the slump were the wrapper-growers of the Connecticut Valley. As a direct result of the antismoking movement, an entire industry and way of life became endangered. Reported the *New*

York Times, "One of the nation's legendary tobacco-growing economies seemed near extinction because demand for its esoteric product was declining along with the popularity of cigars in America."

In the 1920s, 31,000 acres of Shade were under cultivation, and as recently as 1964, 177 Connecticut tobacco farms produced 12 million pounds. Thirty years later the number of farms had been reduced to a dozen, producing 2.3 million pounds in 1994. For a labor-intensive industry in which the cost of growing and processing was $26,000 per acre, as compared to corn's cost of $300 an acre, this loss of market was disastrous. As late as the 1960s, some 8000 acres were devoted to Shade. In 1995 there were only 1700 acres, mostly concentrated in a two-mile-square section of the Connecticut Valley north of Hartford. What once had been a thriving industry increasingly appears to be going the way of dinosaurs.

Noting that cultivation of cigar tobacco had become one of the fastest growing of the state's agricultural activities, the Connecticut Department of Economic Development estimated the value of cigar leaf growing in 1995 at $50 million per year. In assessing total economic benefit to the state at $100 million, the department estimated that had there not been a three-decade drop in public demand for quality cigars the revenues accruing to Connecticut might have been in the billions of dollars. Although growers had attempted to duplicate the variety elsewhere, only three other places in the world were found to have the right soil and climate to replicate what is needed to grow superb wrapper. They are Cameroon, Indonesia, and Cuba. Importations from the former two is expensive. Bringing in tobacco from Communist Cuba, in any form, is prohibited. And efforts to cultivate the Connecticut Shade seed in Virginia, Wisconsin, Florida, and the Carolinas produced an inferior result.

But suddenly, for reasons ascribed to the self-indulgences of the affluent baby-boom generation and the emergence of a white male backlash for a variety of causes, the final decade of the century has experienced an upsurge in consumption of cigars, particularly of the premium brands dependent in large measure upon the singular qualities of Shade wrapper. Although the leaf accounts for no more than 5 percent of a cigar's weight, the wrapper is what gives the cigar the look and most of the taste appreciated both by long-time connoisseurs and by newcomers whose sudden interest in cigars, whether to show off their economic status or to vent sociological grievances, are lending great impetus to the comeback of cigar smoking in the 1990s.

Whatever underlies the surge in popularity of the cigar, the contribution of one man in nurturing the phenomenon cannot be disputed. A confirmed cigar smoker since his college years at the University of Miami, Marvin Shanken at the age of forty-nine and at the height of a successful career in business and publishing decided to promote the cigar as "the Resurrected Symbol of the Rich Life for (Mostly) Men." As the publisher of a successful magazine devoted to fine wine and good food (*The Wine Spectator*), he defied the current logic and advice of experts in the magazine world that there would not be a lucrative market for a publication devoted to cigars.

Introducing *CIGAR Aficionado* in the autumn of 1992, he not only found himself astonished by the immediate success of the venture but also realized that he had become an evangelist for the cigar and the "no-apologies" cheerleader for all the opulent accoutrements of cigar smoking. In addition to the magazine, he promoted Cigar Nights, in which smokers, mostly men, paid $100 to $1000 each to indulge in fine cigars in a hotel banquet room.

The first of the "Big Smoke" evenings, convened in New York in May 1992, attracted 1700 cigar lovers. The second, at the Broadway Ballroom of the Marriott Marquis on November 19, 1992, saw 2500 in attendance at two "sessions" during which they were invited to indulge in the finest cigars of premium makers, and to browse (and buy) the goods of purveyors of classy merchandise. Food and drink came from the top of the line in New York restaurants.

Covering the event for the New York *Daily News,* marketing and advertising correspondent Patricia Winters observed, "In a country where the fashion changed from furs to work boots overnight, these upscale marketers embraced the *Dynasty*-like atmosphere to show off the products of the good life."

The *New York Observer*'s reporter at the next event, "The Big Smoke II," Robert Love, pictured the men attending as "atavists with a cause." Consolidated Cigar's Richard DiMeola smilingly anticipated a 10 to 20 percent increase in business as he declared, "A lot of people have come out of the closet."

Even as The Big Smoke II filled the hotel ballroom with the aroma of fine tobacco, similar extravaganzas had already been planned or scheduled for Chicago, Los Angeles, San Francisco, and Washington, DC.

That there was a market for a magazine devoted to those who like cigars had been demonstrated by the success of *CIGAR Aficionado.* Consequently, in the great tradition of the capitalist system of competitiveness, as well as providing evidence that the First Amendment's guarantee of a free press was alive and well (despite the smoke police), a second magazine made its debut in 1995. Named *Smoke,* it received a lavish send-off in the Bull & Bear restaurant of New York's Waldorf-Astoria Hotel, one of the traditionally cigar-friendly dining rooms in the city.

Whether this upsurge in cigar smoking will be judged by the social historians as fad, renaissance, or revolution remains to be seen. Is this one more orgy of conspicuous consumption? Or does this "comeback" of the cigar indicate a need that runs deeper, even to the spiritual, than mere fleshly pleasures?

If that is the explanation for the dramatic reappearance of the cigar, then thousands of fresh voices are not only echoing Kipling's assertion that "a good cigar is a smoke" but also expressing the intrinsic value assigned to a good cigar by another poet of a century ago. Thomas Hood wrote:

Some sigh for this and that,
My wishes don't go far;
The world may wag at will,
So I have my cigar.

To have my choice among
The toys of life's bazaar,
The deuce may take them all
So I have my cigar.

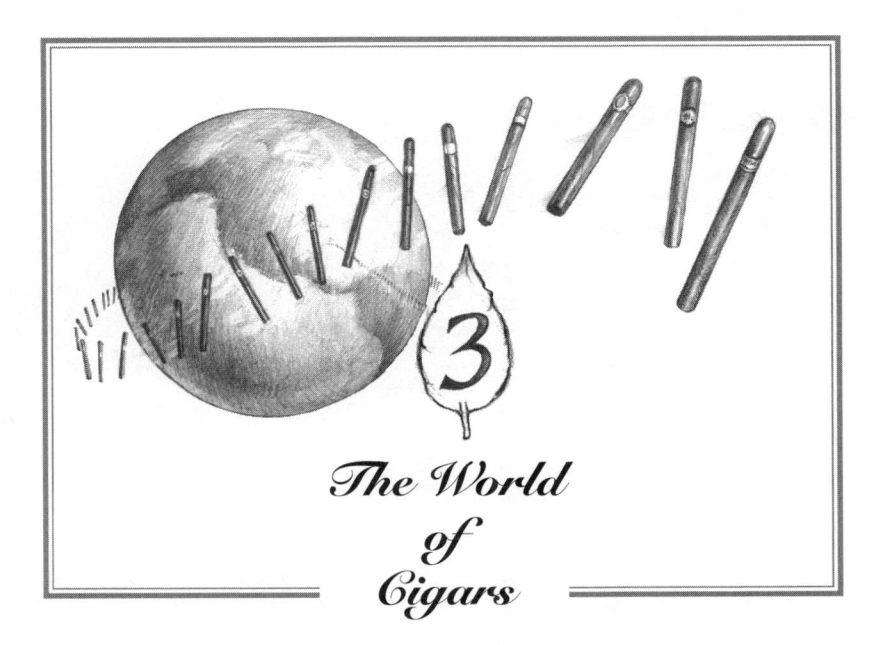

The World of Cigars

LIGHT ME ANOTHER CUBA.
—Rudyard Kipling

Just as champagne is produced in many places in the world but the finest has been associated with the small region of France with whose name the wine was christened, so the connoisseurs of cigars historically pointed to Cuban tobacco as the ultimate in quality. "It is the king of the tobacco products," asserts Zino Davidoff in his classic book on cigars, "and should be treated according to its rank."

Certainly, the colonists of imperial Spain recognized a good thing. Within half a century after Columbus's seafarers came back with the first rudimentary Cuban-made *cigarillo* the city council of Havana had taken steps to ensure that the retail trade in the product would be the sole province of the government. State-owned plantations (*vegas*) were organized with production strictly controlled, along with every other aspect of an industry that would rival and eventually surpass all other

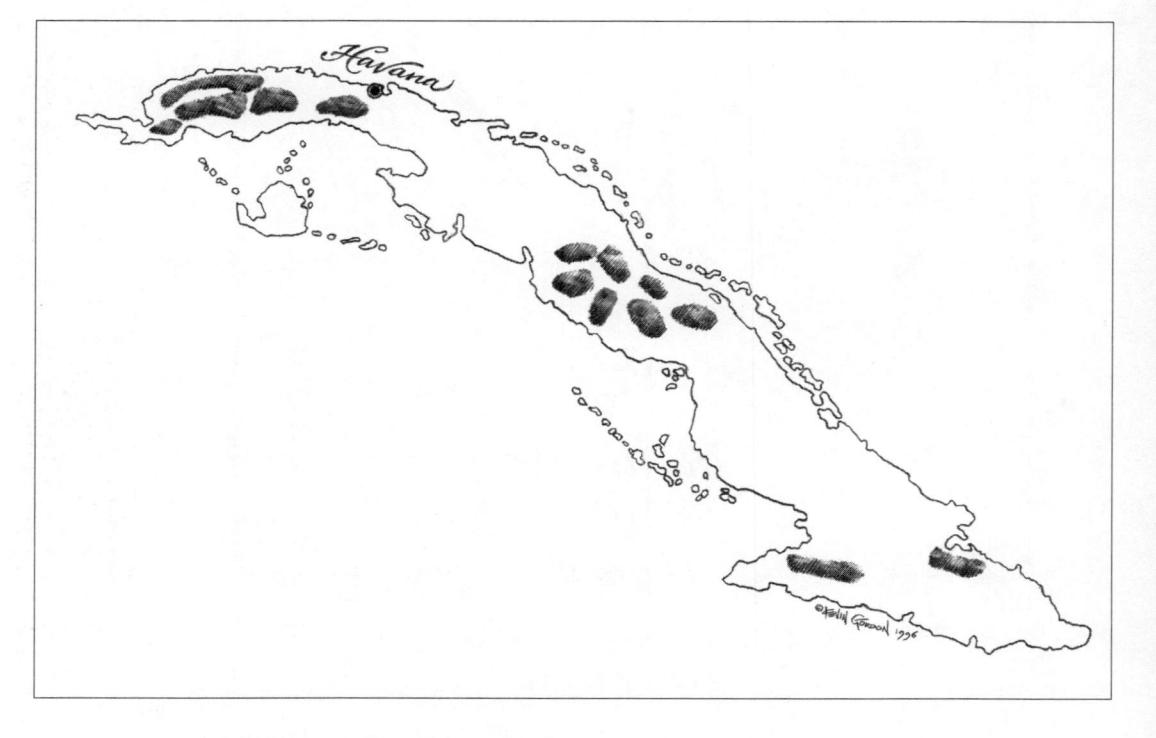

Cuban tobacco growing regions.

forms of agriculture, except sugar. But no matter where it is grown, sugar is sugar, and the prodigious output of Cuban cane fields, while vital to the economy of the island, could never bring Cuba what tobacco afforded—class and prestige.

So powerfully associated with the best tobacco in the world was Cuba that the name of its chief city for exportation quickly became synonymous worldwide with a fine cigar. Havana became the center for exporting Cuban tobacco due to twin blessings of geography: a magnificent harbor and proximity to a region endowed by Nature with a soil superbly suited to growing tobacco.

Described by Zino Davidoff as a "sacred square of ochre-red" earth, the Vuelta Abajo region lies between the mountains and the Caribbean in the westernmost province of Pinar del Rio. Green, lush, and undulating, the area covers about 160 square miles, with most of the tobacco plantations surrounding the towns of San Juan y Martinez and San Luis. Here, where rain falls in the right amounts in the right seasons and sun, shade, and temperature are perfectly attuned to the needs of the tobacco plant, the region's best-known *vegas*, El Corojo and Hoyo de Monterrey, yield wrapper leaves that devotees consider the best in the world.

A second area of Pinar del Rio, Semivuelta, provides leaves that are thicker and with a stronger aroma, but which are reserved primarily for domestic consumption. A third region in the immediate neighborhood of Havana (the Partido) provides product for export. And a markedly inferior (comparatively) tobacco is grown in the provinces at the eastern end of the island, Remedios (also known as Vuelta Arriba) and Oriente.

It is out of the mountains of the latter in 1959 that there emerged a figure of monumental proportions second only to Columbus in the history of Cuba and Cuban tobacco. Clad in an olive green army uniform, lavishly bearded, and rarely photographed without a Havana clutched in his fist, Fidel Castro brought a revolutionary fervor to Cuba that toppled the hated government of the dictator Fulgencio Batista.

Immediately upon Castro's triumphant arrival

When Fidel Castro's revolution brought Communism to Cuba and an alliance with the Soviet Union, United States retaliation in the form of an embargo on importation of Havana cigars led directly to an exodus of cuban cigar makers and the growth of a competition in premium cigar manufacturing in the Dominican Republic, Honduras and other Latin American countries. American plans to eliminate Castro included a plot by the Central Intelligence Agency to kill him by poisoning his cigars, but the scheme was not attempted. Some people believe these plans provoked Castro into ordering the assassination of President John F. Kennedy in 1963. Courtesy of New York Public Library in the capital, Havana changed dramatically. Swept aside was the city of sin that had flourished under Batista. For decades the splendid capital had attracted literary luminaries such as Ernest Hemingway and Graham Greene, whose books touted its fleshly fascinations and intrigues; a generation of American gangsters that included Lucky Luciano, Bugsy Siegel, and Meyer Lansky; movie stars; hordes of sensation-seeking tourists; and, of course, true lovers of fine cigars. Suddenly, an island that since Columbus's arrival was called "Pearl of the Antilles" was now looked upon aghast and with alarm while it was bitterly denounced as a dreaded "Red toehold in the Western Hemisphere" and "a Communist threat ninety miles from Miami."

Deciding that this situation was not tolerable, the Eisenhower administration drew up plans for the ouster of Castro from Cuba. When John F. Kennedy was elected in 1960, plans to land Cuban exiles at the Bay of Pigs, covertly supported by the Central Intelligence Agency and elements of the U.S. military, were passed to his administration. Only partially implemented, the landings resulted in disastrous defeat in the spring of 1961. Angered by the effort to depose him, Castro strengthened his ties to the Soviets. A year and a half later the alliance provoked the Cuban Missile Crisis, driving the world to the brink of nuclear war.

American retaliation against Castro took the form of an economic embargo, but, according to JFK's press secretary in 1961, Pierre Salinger, not until Kennedy, a smoker of Cuban cigars, assured himself of a stockpile of his favorite Havanas. Called into the Oval Office one afternoon, Salinger was ordered to obtain a thousand Petit Upmanns by the next morning. He returned and proudly reported completion of the assignment. With a satisfied smile, Kennedy opened his desk, took out a long sheet of paper, and signed his name to it, therewith imposing by the stroke of his pen an embargo on all imports of Cuban cigars that would remain in effect through four decades.

Unless they were willing to defy the law, the effect on American smokers was painful in the extreme. And the embargo and subsequent events in the years of the Cold War produced suffering for Cubans that proved far worse. In the aftermath of the collapse of Soviet Communism, Cuba lost its chief economic market—the USSR. The removal of this mainstay, combined with the strangling effects of the American embargo on almost all Cuban goods, left the island a virtual financial derelict. Especially affected was the tobacco industry. Added to the loss of Soviet fiscal underpinning was an inability to replace aging equipment and to obtain fuel, pesticides, and the all-important cloth for shading precious leaves. Nor did weather help. Hurricanes wreaked havoc in tobacco-growing regions. These conditions led to a significant decline in export-quality cigars, from 100 million a year in the 1980s, when the Soviet Union was still in existence, to half that output since the demise of Moscow in 1989 as Cuba's economic savior.

Another aspect of the soured relations between the United States and Castro's Cuba was an outflow of anti-Communist Cubans—including many of Cuba's finest artisans in the making of cigars—to the United States and to other Latin American countries. The exodus created an explosion of production of Cuban-quality cigars that soon rivaled and competed with Cuba's output. Among the many famous Cuban cigar barons who fled and went into business elsewhere, some appropriated such famous Cuban brands as Partagas, H. Upmann, and Montecristo.

With this new source, many premium-cigar smokers wondered if true Cuban cigars could regain their pre-Castro status. Richard DiMeola of Consolidated Cigar, a company in direct competition with Cuban cigars, faulted them for often being harsh and hard to keep lit, as well as leaving an unpleasant acidic feeling in the chest. Norman F. Sharp, president of the Cigar Association of America, representing manufacturers and importers, expressed the view that with new cigars of Cuban quality available from numerous other sources "the mystique is gone."

When *USA Today* asked, "Do Cuban cigars merit the adoration? Are they worth prices as high as $40 a cigar?" Marvin Shanken, founder, publisher, and editor of *CIGAR Aficionado,* retorted, "A lot of countries make excellent cigars. Cuba doesn't have the monopoly. But if you want a full, rich, flavorful cigar with a bit of spice, *that* is the Cuban contribution."

Decades before *USA Today* posed what lovers of Cuban cigars undoubtedly regarded as an impertinence and before the expression of the proposition that the "mystique" of Cuban cigars had been dispelled, one of the world's foremost champions of the Havana, Zino Davidoff, declared that "all great smokers discovered long ago the irreplaceable virtues of this magic island: its geology, wind, water, and miraculous soil."

Another writer called the Vuelta Abajo "a natural hothouse, just as the whole island of Cuba is a natural humidor." The area surrounding Havana includes plantations likened to the legendary wine estates of Latour and Lafitte in France and glorified by one writer for *CIGAR Aficionado* magazine as having "similar God-given attributes that no other places in the world can match, enabling them to produce fabulous crops."

Arguably the most favored by Nature of the government-owned tobacco farms of the Vuelta Abajo, with ideal conditions for the cultivation of perfect wrapper leaf, is the plantation called El Corojo. A few miles from San Luis y Martinez, it extends over 395 acres and employs around six hundred people to work the fields and maintain the barns. As did all the farms in Cuba, it began as a family enterprise and remained so until Castro's revolution communized the island's tobacco industry. The result was to drive the heirs of the founder, Diego Rodriguez, from Cuba to the United States. But the land remained behind, of course, still producing, despite the hard times that ultimately befell the Cuban tobacco industry under Communism, the superb wrapper leaf that is regarded by many as the best in the world—Cohiba.

Lauded for its gloriously rich aromas and flavors of coffee and chocolate, Cohiba has been called the Cadillac of premium cigars. Distinguished by its bright yellow, white, and black band, it has become—the embargo notwithstanding—a status symbol of the cigar-smoking rich and famous. Certainly, a healthy wallet is necessary to be able to light up one of six Cohiba varieties: Lancero, Esplendido, Coronas Especial, Robusto, Exquisito, and Panatela. The least expensive, the 4½-inch, 26-ring-gauge Panatela, sold in 1995 for $8.90. The 5-inch, 36-ring-gauge Exquisito cost $12.20. And the 38-ring-gauge, 6- to 7½-inch Coronas Especial and Lancero went for $21.80.

Although quality and reputation have always been calculated in the price of Cohibas, just as important in fixing the retail cost is quantity. For Cohibas the average annual output for all varieties in the 1990s was around 3½ million. That amounts to roughly one-third of the productivity of a major cigar factory.

Because of the ban on importing Cuban cigars to the United States, those seeking to buy the prized Cohibas also have to factor in the expenses of travel to cities, such as London, where the cigars are readily available in tony emporiums that include Davidoff of London, J.J. Fox, (Cigar Merchants) Ltd., Robert Lewis (St. James's) Ltd., Walter Thurgood, Desmond Sautter Ltd., and the cigar counters of Britain's most exclusive department store, Harrods.

Before the finished Cohibas reach these purveyors to pass into the fingers of their avid purchasers, their prized tobacco will have gone through the traditional processes of manufacture in the rolling rooms around and in Havana. To many connoisseurs each factory, signified by a code number on the cigar box, is a key to the quality of the cigars within. The knowing buyer recognizes these export factories:

JM	H. Upmann
FR	La Corona
BM	Romeo y Julieta
FPG	Partagas
HM	El Rey del Mundo
EL	El Laguito

The latter is a villa that stands on a hill in Havana. Inside its rolling rooms work hundreds of men and women, turning out cigars in much the same manner as generations of Cubans before them. The procedure is the same in all the factories. In the November 22, 1994, issue of *USA Today*, Marco R. della Cava on a visit to the Partagas factory in Havana observed row after row of cigar makers seated like schoolchildren at old, battered, wooden desks. Lips sealed and fingers flying, they were tobacco artisans "lost in a trance generations old."

Presumably, their children and their children's children will continue to do so as long as there are those who wish to smoke Cuban cigars and speak of them in terms that, except for extravagances of advertising, are not usually applied to things man-made. One does not expect to hear of the mystique of the washing machine, TV set, or home computer. Should builders of these modern amenities be described as doing their work "in a trance generations old," let the buyer beware. And when have the virtues of having been grown in some magical place blessed by geology, wind, water, and miraculous soil been attributed to corn and wheat?

To what other commodities have so many poets waxed as eloquently as they have of the cigar? For what worldly thing would a man abandon his wife, as did the husband in Kipling's poem when forced to choose between her and his Havanas?

Yet Cuba is not and never has been the only source of fine cigars. Not far away lies an island divided into two countries—Haiti, and the one that would arise as the chief rival of Cuba in the world of cigars.

Dominican Republic

It was at this place in 1492, before setting foot in Cuba, that Christopher Columbus exclaimed, "The mountain ranges, the hills, the valleys, and their fields are strikingly beautiful. The soil is fertile."

Though he did not know it, the admiral was describing cigar

The Dominican Republic's cigar industry is concentrated around the capital.

country. Five hundred years after he named the island "Hispaniola," the nation that occupies its eastern half is a home to many of the world's largest cigar makers outside Cuba. They are General Cigar, Consolidated Cigar, Tabacos Dominicanas, Matasa, and Arturo Fuente. They produce premium brands with the bulk of their supply earmarked for the market in the United States, a market enhanced by the Cuban embargo. Indeed, it was the communization of Cuban agriculture that drove some of Cuba's finest cigar-making families into exile in the Dominican Republic, other Latin American countries, and cities in the United States, especially in and around Miami, Florida. When they left they carried with them, to the consternation of Cuba, many of the most illustrious names in the lore and legend of the cigar.

Located around Santiago in the Cibao River valley, the Dominican Republic's primary leaf cultivation region offers exactly the environment of heat and humidity required to produce premium leaf. Unlike the Vuelta Abajo of Cuba, the Dominican Republic does not grow top-quality wrapper. Its factories rely on imports from Cameroon, Nicaragua, Brazil, Mexico, Ecuador, and Connecticut. The domestic supply of binder and filler is augmented by imports from many of the same countries, plus Java in the East Indies.

Brands produced include Avo Uvezian, Black Watch, Bolivar, Canaria d'Oro, Casa Blanca, Davidoff, Don Diego, Dunhill, Griffin's, H. Upmann, Henry Clay, Jose Benito, Juan Clemente, Knockando, La Corona, Macanudo, Montecruz, Montesino, Partagas, Paul Garmirian, Pleiades, Por Lorranaga, Primo del Rey, Quorum, Ramon Allones, Romeo y Julieta, Royal Dominicana, Royal Jamaica, Santa Damiana, Shakespeare, Special Coronas, Special Jamaicans, and Tresado.

Those produced by Consolidated Cigar appear under the auspices of the company's premium-cigar wing, Tabacalera de Garcia, established in the Dominican Republic after Consolidated's parent company, Gulf & Western Corporation, withdrew operations from the Canary Islands in 1980. Eight years later Consolidated was taken over by Revlon, headed by cigar connoisseur Ronald Perelman. As of 1995 it was exporting 18 million cigars a year by the brand names of H. Upmann, Henry Clay, Don Diego, Primo del Rey, and Royal Jamaica (not made in Jamaica). It also provides the entire line of Dunhill Dominicans, including the prized Montecruz.

General Cigar makes Macanudo, Partagas, Canaria d'Oro, and Black Watch. Its vice president of premium-cigar manufacturing, Benjamin Menendez, brought to the company the experience of his family of Cuban cigar artisans in the crafting of H. Upmann and Montecristo brands. They decamped from Cuba as Castro came to power in 1959.

One of the oldest Dominican producers is A. Fuente, founded in the late nineteenth century. Having gotten started in cigar making in Cuba, Don Arturo Fuente left the country with little money but treasure nonetheless in the form of expertise in the art of making fine cigars. The company he created in 1912 and passed to his heirs remains one of the main family-owned cigar enterprises. In the largest factory making handmades, they turn out 18 million cigars a year that are well constructed with medium to full flavor in a choice of *maduro* wrappers. They range in size from the 9-inch Hemingway Masterpiece and the 8¹/₂-inch Canones to the 4-inch Hemingway Short Story.

That Don Carlos named cigars after Ernest Hemingway is a reflection of his conviction that Hemingway was "a man devoted to the good life, a man who appreciated great cigars and admired the difficult craft of making them, as he did all dignified and hard-won triumphs of skill." Advertised by the company as *"un puro autentico"* (an authentic cigar), Hemingways are packaged in special handmade cedar boxes.

Two families who also found Communist Cuba inhospitable, the Quesadas and Sosas, arrived in Miami in 1961 searching for a home for their separate long-established tobacco operations, but they soon decided to merge and move to the Dominican Republic. The result was the Fonseca. Grown in the Cibao valley and wrapped with Connecticut Shade, it is available in six sizes: Petit Corona, Robusto, Classic Corona, Corona Gorda, the Triangular (with a conical shape), and the formidable Churchill.

Another partnership in Dominican cigar making began when Angel LaMadrid Cuesta, who had rolled his first cigar in 1884, and Peregrino Rey combined their passions for cigar making and their names to produce Cuesta Rey cigars. Elegantly packed in cedar cabinets of fifteen to twenty-five, they range from 8¹/₂ to 6¹/₂ inches in length and ring gauges between 36 and 52.

For the Quesada family the business of cigars began when they owned a bakery and were paid by a customer with tobacco. As a result of that unique legacy, Manuel Quesada found himself a century and a

THE
WORLD
OF
CIGARS

53

quarter later at the head of a firm producing an annual total of 5½ million Matasa, Finck, Romeo y Julieta, Jose Benito, and Santa Maria cigars.

When Ramon Cifuentes left Cuba in 1960 he had $100 and all the knowledge and experience gained in making Partagas cigars. Thirty years later an advertising campaign for the Partagas that his family continued to make in the Dominican Republic featured a picture taken of him just after he left his homeland, along with his words, "Fidel Castro thought I had left Cuba with only the clothes on my back. But my secrets were locked in my heart." Those secrets resulted in the family's new Partagas brand becoming one of the world's best-selling premium cigars and a powerful rival of Macanudo in popularity in the United States.

These and other Dominican operations produced exports to the United States in the 1990s totaling more than 50 million a year, about half of the demand of the U.S. market for premium cigars. Whether that output might be sustained remains to be seen if, as premium-cigar lovers devoutly wish and hope, the ban on importation of Cuban cigars were ended.

Honduras

Second only to the Dominican Republic in its exports to the United States in the 1990s, Honduras, in Central America, shipped more than 40 million from factories dispersed around the country, from the hot, coastal plains around San Pedro Sula to the cooler mountains and hills of Santa Rosa de Copán and Danlí. As in the Dominican Republic, the status of the Honduran industry received a tremendous boost upon the arrival of anti-Castro Cuban refugees in the 1960s. The trade developed as both family-based and corporate enterprises. Among the latter were Consolidated Cigar and U.S. Tobacco company's Central American Cigars. Firms with strong associations with individuals and families include Tabacos Plasencia, Honduras American Tobacco, Villazon, and Tabacos Flor de Copán.

Despite the Cuban roots of so many of the growers and manufacturers, they boast with all the nationalistic fervor of people who settle in a new country that their cigars are as fine as any coming from Cuba. Part of the claim to equality lies in the fact that the Honduran product has been produced from seed brought from Cuba.

Yet some claim that the full-flavored cigars of Honduras are actually better than Havanas. "Honduran cigars," said one advocate, "are what people smoke when they grow up."

Representative Honduran premium cigars are Baccarat, Bances, Don Mateo, Don Ramos, Don Tomas, El Rey del Mundo, Excalibur, Hoyo de Monterrey, J.R. Ultimate, La Invicta, La Primadora, Mocha, Punch, Riata, and Zino.

Jamaica

A British colony in the West Indies for more than three centuries, Jamaica gained its independence in 1962 and also found itself a beneficiary of the exodus of cigar craftsmen from Cuba. Among the island's handmades are: Chevere, Jamaica Bay, Jamaica Gem, Jamaica Gold, Jamaican Club, Jamaican Kings, Jamaican Silky, Jamaican Supreme, Macanudo, Mario Palomino, Old Fashioned, Old Harbour, Santa Cruz, Temple Hall, and Whitehall.

Mexico

Bordering the Gulf of Mexico, but four thousand feet above sea level, the lush San Andrés Valley was growing tobacco long before the arrival of Spanish *conquistadores*. It was here that local priests led the worship of deities by smoking long tubes of the leaves of the abundant tobacco plant. To that ancient people the clouds of the sky were believed to be smoke produced by gods as they enjoyed tobacco. Shooting stars were thought to be tobacco embers falling to earth.

Unfortunately, this perception of tobacco's place in life and heaven fell victim to the vagaries of human history. The tale of tobacco in Mexico is as troubled as the country's frequently tempestuous political past, including a revolution in 1910 that broke up long-established, large cigar estates of wealthy families. But it was subsequent upheavals outside Mexico that fostered development of its modern cigar trade. Revolt against the dictator Sukarno in Indonesia in 1949 created an exodus of Dutch cigar makers to Mexico, bringing with them Sumatran seed that is world-renowned for producing large, velvety leaves that are ideal as wrapper. This influx was followed by Cubans fleeing Castro in the 1960s. They brought with them unparalleled skills as makers of cigars and a determination to benefit from the embargo on imports from Cuba by meeting the demands of the Havana-starved smokers in the United States.

For Jorge Ortiz Alvarez, manager of Tabacos Santa Clara, the arrival of Cuban refugees was a defining moment; it changed the way Mexican growers and marketers presented their cigars to the world. "We started to choose tobacco differently," he explains. "We made changes to meet a market that was more demanding."

A major result of the introduction of Sumatran seed was the elimination of the need for Mexican manufacturers to import wrapper from their previous suppliers in Indonesia and the Connecticut Valley. This meant the product could be made entirely in Mexico. Some popular brands are Mocambo and Santa Clara and Consolidated Cigar's Matacan. These are well made but not as tightly rolled as are most premium cigars. They draw well, and provide a medium to full flavor that is a bit sweet and spicy. They range in length/ring from No. 1's 7½ inches /50 to No. 9's 5/32.

Among the popular Mexican brands are Aromas de San Andreas, Cruz Real, El Beso, Hoja de Mexicali, Hoja de Oro, Kingstown, Matacan, Mexican Emperador, Mocambo, Santa Clara "1830," Sancho Panza, and Veracruz.

One of the brands created in Mexico following the arrival of the Cuban refugees would become what is arguably the best known. It is Consolidated Cigar's Te-Amo. A variety of names have been given to the cigars made at the Matacapan Tabacos factory in the heart of the San Andrés valley. Generally they are medium-flavored and tightly rolled cigars available in a choice of coarse, light brown *madura* wrappers.

Encouraged and financed by New York businessmen, makers of Te-Amo quickly discovered that their cigar had a faithful following among managers and workers of New York City's bustling garment district. Although the population within the fashion industry of the city has diminished since the 1970s, echoes of the immense popularity of the brand can still be found. Te-Amo signs still adorn many of the corner newsstands and stores that purvey tobacco to the men of a metropolis that has always been a mecca for smokers.

The United States

When Vice President Marshall made his famous off-the-cuff remark, that what America needed was a "good five-cent cigar," the country was on the brink of the decade that would become notorious as "the Roaring Twenties." The United States was also a nation that by then had fallen in love with the cigar.

In "the Gay Nineties," more than 4 billion cigars were sold annually. By 1904 smokers in the United States spent sixty cents out of each tobacco-dollar on cigars but only a nickel for cigarettes. In 1920 more than 8 billion cigars were sold. Much of this growth in popularity was the result of two peculiarly American proclivities—mechanization and salesmanship.

The introduction of machines to make cigars had occurred in the 1880s with the invention of an apparatus to eliminate costly hand operations. It was a wooden mold for pressing tobacco into bunches. This led, inevitably, to machines capable of stemming, cutting, and wrapping. One of the inventors was the theatrical impresario Oscar Hammerstein. He patented a cigar-making machine in 1883. By the end of the century technology had advanced so far as to permit both the mass production and the mass marketing of domestically made cigars.

Enter one of the most colorful characters in American lore, the tobacco "drummer." This individual was enchantingly depicted by Jerome Brooks in *The Mighty Leaf*:

This expansive, hearty character, perhaps influenced by the showmanship of the great P.T. Barnum, was distinctively arrayed in high hat, frock-tail, and bright waistcoat made more glaring by a conspicuous display of jewelry proper to a congenial man, member of the most popular lodges. He was not only redolent of the odoriferous trade he represented; he exuded fellowship, for he was a dispenser of an article of congeniality.

For comedian W. C. Fields, the basic ingredients of a great gag were his straw hat, white gloves, cane, and stogie. He credited his successful career to a daily consumption of whiskey and cigars that began in boyhood. Courtesy of New York Public Library

Except for the gaudy attire, the salesmen encountered in the cigar stores of America a century later are from the same mold, for the one thing that the improved technology and marketing of cigars has not changed is their innate ability to immediately invoke a mood of relaxation and affability. Perhaps that is why so many comedians and other entertainers have integrated a cigar into their acts, from W.C. Fields, George Burns, and Groucho Marx cavorting on vaudeville stages to David Letterman on late-night television.

The cigar also figured into the personal history of a giant in the business of American entertainment. He was William S. Paley, the son of Samuel Paley, founder of the family's Congress Cigar Company of Chicago. It produced the La Palina, a variation on the family name. Its band featured a picture of Mrs. Paley.

When the enterprise was moved to Philadelphia the teenage Bill became involved in its operations by hiring new employees and traveling to Cuba to acquire tobacco for the firm's ultramodern factory. It and six other operations in several eastern states produced half a million a day of what Paley advertisements touted as "America's largest selling high-grade cigar." The sales later rose to close to a million and a half a day, with profits more than doubling in the 1920s. Mounting family resources soon provided Bill Paley with the financing to acquire a radio station in Philadelphia (WCAU). It became the flagship of the radio network that would evolve into the radio and TV broadcasting, recording, and entertainment goliath, CBS, Inc.

Among cigar makers that competed with the Paley family in the cigar business during the Roaring Twenties were firms that had been built on the American male's demand for tobacco in the form of cigars. Most of these were not the painstakingly hand-rolled, expensive products associated with the Caribbean. The majority of the domestic output came from machines and sold inexpensively under brand names that became as familiar to Americans as Ford, Coca-Cola, and Maxwell House. The average cigar smoker walked into his neighborhood tobacconist and asked for a Robert Burns, White Owl, Phillies, La Corona, El Producto, Garcia y Vega, or Optimo.

But the decade that witnessed the advent of Prohibition and the speakeasy also saw a decline in cigar smoking in favor of the cigarette. Between 1918 and 1928 the total production of cigarettes in the United

States more than doubled. Much of the increase in consumption is because women had begun to smoke. The arrival on the social scene of a cigarette-smoking "flapper" who danced to jazz music marked a fundamental shift in American social mores and affected the fate of the cigar.

The famed historian of the 1920s Frederick Lewis Allen wrote in *Only Yesterday*:

> Part of this increase [in cigarettes] was doubtless due to the death of the one-time masculine prejudice against the cigarette as unmanly. . . . Part of it was attributable to the fact that the convenience of the cigarette made the masculine smoker consume more tobacco than in the days when he preferred a cigar or pipe. . . . Hosts who laid in a stock of cigars for their male guests often found them untouched.

The custom of "the ladies" withdrawing from the dining room after dinner to leave the men with their "port and cigars" was on the way to becoming a quaint feature of "period" movies and television shows, primarily produced in Britain.

Thus began a persistent and steady decline in the status of the cigar that has continued for most of the balance of the century, only to rebound somewhat now in the 1990s perhaps, ironically, as a form of rebellion by more and more men against further incursions into the provinces of masculinity by women. Certainly, nothing had symbolized that manly realm in the previous five hundred years more than the cigar. However, as a consequence of the cigarette's domination of the American tobacco industry since the 1920s, men in the United States who chose to express their revolutionary fervor, or, in Marvin Shanken's phrase, the "outlaw" in their nature, had to look for the ultimate symbol of newfound assertiveness—the premium cigar—among fewer and fewer firms daring enough to continue making expensive cigars in such a diminishing market.

By 1995 there remained only one cigar-making company in the place where Israel Putnam had envisioned a glorious future in the manufacture of cigars. A century and a third later the lone exponent of the cigar in Connecticut is F.D. Grave and Son. But the line of cigars that the firm markets is not actually made in the Nutmeg State. The manufacturing is contracted out to a factory in Pennsylvania, with business aspects of the operation run from company headquarters in New Haven.

Located on State Street, the original Grave factory, opened in 1901, was hailed as one of most substantial, modern, and up-to-date cigar factories in this or any other country. But the economics of the cigar trade forced the closing of the manufacturing operation in favor of the less expensive environs of Pennsylvania. At the same time, the family-owned company reduced its line of cigars from a high of twenty-two to ten. Seven of these were marketed under the Muniemaker brand, which had been acquired from Osterweis & Sons in 1954.

What does not change in the making of Grave cigars, however, is the wrapper. The sole supply is still obtained from the nearby farms of the Connecticut River Valley.

With the decline in domestic manufacture of premium cigars in the 1930s and the limiting of operation by the great U.S. tobacco firms to cigars produced on high-tech machinery for a downscale market, an American citizen looking for a premium smoke turned to imports from countries that benefited from the influx of makers who had honed the skills of hand-rolling cigars in Cuba. But not all had settled in the Dominican Republic, Honduras, and Mexico. Many of the best of Cuba's artisans elected to make the ninety-mile trip to the United States. Landing in Florida, they turned sections of Miami, Tampa, and other cities in the Sunshine State into "Little Havanas."

One of those who brought cigar-making talents to Florida was Ernesto Carillo. In a series of small stores, his factory (*fabrica*) turned out La Gloria Cubana cigars with the names Gloria, Corona Gorda,

Gloria Extra, Medaille d'Oro No. 1, Charlemagne, Soberano, Wavell, Double Corona, and Torpedo No. 1. They range in length from 5½ inches with a ring gauge of 43 (La Gloria Cubana) to the 7-inch, 50-ring, triangular-shaped Torpedo. As a member of a family that started in the cigar trade in Cuba in their El Credito Cigars firm (a name they carried with them to America), Ernesto Carillo proudly insists, "My cigars are some of the closest cigars to Cuban ones."

His claim surely would be disputed by many other Floridian cigar makers who also trace their lineage to Cuba. Certainly, a dissent could be expected from a city on Florida's Gulf Coast. For the first half of the twentieth century, Tampa reigned as the cigar capital of the world. Beginning with the opening of the Flor de Sanchez & Haya company in the late nineteenth century, the industry flourished to the point where its factories turned out more Havana-quality cigars than did Cuba itself. But with the upsurge of production in Latin America in the 1960s by Cuban expatriates, many of Tampa's largest manufacturers shifted operations so as to benefit from the availability of the Cuban exiles, as well as lower labor costs, in countries to which they had emigrated in large numbers.

Among the producers who looked to the Dominican Republic were Corral, Wodiska, where millions of Havana Bering and Spanish Colonials had been made; Perfecto Garcia; the Morgan Company; Arturo Fuente; Gradiaz-Annis, manufacturer of the popular Gold Label; and one of the biggest of Tampa's historic tobacco makers, M & N Standard. Known as "the Home of Cuesta Rey Cigars," M & N shifted its premium line to the Dominican Republic and Honduras, leaving its machine-made operations to produce its lower priced line of Rigoletto and Luis Martinez in Tampa.

One of the oldest surviving manufacturers in the United States, M & N was founded in 1895 by J.C. Newman in Cleveland, Ohio. When a recession forced a merger with the Mendelsohn company, also of Cleveland, in 1921, the firm had ridden tides of cigar popularity from the crest at the turn of the century to its ebb between the two World Wars and afterward, then back to a crest in the 1990s. In the course of these ups and downs the company was the first to package cigars in cellophane instead of foil.

Having moved to Tampa following World War II, to be closer to the source of Cuban tobacco, M & N (now owned entirely by the Newman family) acquired the Cuesta Rey brand in 1958 and promoted its sale in supermarkets and drugstores until it became one of the most popular cigars in the United States.

In its own operations, administered from Tampa, and through a joint venture with the Fuente family (FANCO), the firm in 1994 shipped around 40 million machine-made cigars and approximately 25 million hand-rolled.

A plant that stayed in Tampa was the Villazon factory, "Home of the Bances Cigars." Owned by Frank Llaneza and Tino Gonzales, it purveyed Honduran-based J. R. Ultimates, Rey del Mundo, Consuegra, Belinda, Hoyo de Monterrey, and Punch.

Another source of handmade cigars in the "Little Havanas" of Florida and other cities on the East Coast (a few can be found in California) is the individual cigar maker who runs a factory that is also the store and often a home. These small operations are called *chinchales* ("sweatshops"). Their proprietors are artisans who fled from Cuba to go into business on their own, mostly in Miami and Tampa, and in Union City, New Jersey.

Benefits of buying from a *chinchale* are freshness and uniqueness. The trade-off can be a lack of the consistency that comes with products of larger businesses. The cigar smoker who expects his purchases to be uniform in size, color, and construction, or boxed in elegant cedar cabinets and with beautiful collectible bands, should look elsewhere. Nor are these individualistic cigars necessarily a better buy in terms of price. Some can turn out to be not worth the cost, no matter how attractive the savings might have seemed.

While all these alternatives serve to placate the world's largest market for Cuban cigars, Americans confronting the dawn of the third millennium continue to wait in hope for an end to the four-decade-old embargo on the real thing.

The World's Other Cigars

Although the Western Hemisphere is the cradle of tobacco and the chief supplier of cigars, both have been produced elsewhere, and those have their enthusiasts, too. As has been noted, the explorers, adventurers, and conquerors who followed in Columbus's wake promptly transported American tobacco as plant and seed to their homelands in the hope that it could be transplanted and cultivated.

Soon, smoking of tobacco as cigars and in pipes was spreading like wildfire as mariners and merchants on horseback plied trade routes from Spain, Portugal, England, and the Netherlands to the Orient and Africa. But in addition to indoctrinating peoples of foreign lands into the pleasures of smoking, these early wayfarers sought to guarantee themselves ample supplies of the leaf by planting tobacco wherever they went. Cultivation was started in the Philippines around 1575 and by the early 1700s tobacco had taken root in China, where it was called "smoke blossom," "herb of amiability," and "herb of discernment"; in Macao; Korea; Mongolia; eastern Siberia; Tibet; and Turkistan. Portuguese and Dutch colonists saw that tobacco found its way to Africa. By the time King James I took the throne of England it could be said, as it was by one of James's courtiers, "O sovereign tobacco!"

Smoking was not only prevalent throughout the world, writes historian James Brooks, but it was also the most distinctive of the social customs newly acquired by man. It withstood savage abuses, prohibition and persecution and economic strain, but it had become a comfortable daily routine in most places around the globe. "The trade in tobacco, expanding at a rapid rate," writes Brooks, "became almost the greatest in international commerce. For the market had become the inhabited world."

So rampant was tobacco that in 1823 in his poem *The Island* Lord Byron wrote:

> *Sublime tobacco! which from east to west*
> *Cheers the tar's labour or the Turkman's rest;*
> *Which on the Moslem's ottoman divides*
> *His hours, and rivals opium and his brides;*
> *Magnificent in Stamboul, but less grand,*
> *Though not less loved, in Wapping or the Strand;*
> *Divine in hookas, glorious in pipe.*
> *When tipp'd with amber, mellow, rich and ripe;*
> *Like other charmers, wooing the caress*
> *More dazzling when daring in full dress;*
> *Yet true lovers more admire by far*
> *Thy naked beauties—give me a cigar!*

In addition to declaring that "a woman is only a woman, but a good cigar is a smoke," Rudyard Kipling happily proclaimed that he had his choice of a Larranaga, a Partagas, a Henry Clay, and "a harem of dusky beauties, fifty tied in a string."

While the heart of the world of cigars was the West Indies, tobacco flourished wherever the climate was amenable to cultivation. Sailors introduced tobacco to the Canary Islands and created a cigar-making industry whose modern brands include Condale, Penamil, Victoria, and Dunhill. Among the first of the non–Western Hemisphere lands to emerge as a rival was Sumatra. The leaf produced is thin, silky, of excellent flavor, and ideal as wrapper. Two pounds can make one thousand cigars, compared to five to ten pounds of Connecticut leaf. By 1900 more than 5 million pounds were being imported a year. This prompted worried Connecticut growers to experiment with ways to improve their product. That they succeeded is evident: Today the shade-grown Connecticut Valley product is regarded by many as among the best in the world.

Because Sumatra lies in the rich East Indies, it became one of the most important of the colonies acquired by the Netherlands. The second largest of the islands that constitute the present nation of Indonesia, Sumatra had its share of western visitors before the Dutch came, including Marco Polo, the Portuguese, and the British. The Dutch arrived in 1596 and stayed through the end of the World War II.

Quick to recognize that tobacco flourished in the island's hot, wet climate, Dutch merchants soon turned a tidy profit in trading it. In the process they elevated Sumatra and other Dutch East Indian holdings, including nearby Java, high into the rankings of significant places in the world of fine cigars and placed the Dutch among the ranks of connoisseurs and makers of cigars. Among the Netherlands brands (primarily dry-cured and machine-made) are Agio, Davidoff small cigars, Henri Winterman, Schimmelpennick, Panter, Willem II, and Zino. Dutch Treats, however, are made in the United States.

Other European countries with cigar industries are Germany, Belgium, Switzerland, Italy, Portugal, and, of course, the country that started it all.

Spain

Imagine a place where cigar smoking is not only allowed, but also encouraged; where Cuban cigars are as easily attainable as a pack of chewing gum; where the person next to you does not scowl when you put a cigar to your lips but instead offers you a light. That's today in Spain.

Cigar smoking is as much a part of Spanish culture as the bullfight and the flamenco. At the Plaza de Toros in Madrid you will find scores of vendors in colorful stalls selling every kind of Havana from Cohiba Lanceros to Montecristo No. 3.

During the springtime festival of San Isidro, when there is a bullfight every day for a month, the Plaza is sold out every afternoon. Aficionados with their pockets bulging with premium smokes enjoy not just the performances of Spain's top matadors but also the finest cigars in the world. About two-thirds of the more than 35,000 spectators are men and about 90 percent of them enjoy cigars. Great clouds of smoke billow from the circular stadium.

Just as Spanish *machismo* has room for women bullfighters, the pleasures of the *puro* are being enjoyed by the ladies of Spain. A raven-haired señorita puffing on a long cigar is now as common as the hordes of young American males in their white clothes and red scarves running with the bulls in Pamplona and acting as if they were young Hemingways either on the way to writing their version of *The Sun Also Rises* or looking to give a cigar band as a memento to another Ava Gardner.

The cigar also reaches into the bullring. When a matador's performance so pleases the spectators that they demand that he take a triumphal lap around the ring to receive their accolades, he is showered with men's hats, women's shawls, and a cascade of cigars. The matador's assistants toss back the hats and shawls. They keep the cigars.

On any street, in parks and in crowded restaurants and bars, groups of boisterous, lusty men also smoke Spanish-made cigars whose smoke is as distinctive as the Madrileño accent. But the provocative image from the opera *Carmen*, of fiery women rolling cigars in their Seville factory, has been replaced with that of modern facilities in the north of Spain and the Canary Islands. Brands include Farias, Peñamil, Condal, and Goya. The Spanish monopoly, Tabacalera, enjoys average annual sales of $300 million.

Spain is also the world's largest importer of Cuban cigars. More than 60 percent of Cuban handmades are sold at the lowest prices outside of Cuba, primarily because the Spanish government imposes the lowest taxes on tobacco products in Europe.

Asia

The cigar reaches to the most distant places in the world. As an English surgeon, John Fryer, during his travels to India between 1669 and 1679, was tramping through a "poor and miserable town," he observed inhabitants "smoke their tobacco after a very mean but I judge original manner: the leaf rolled up and light one end holding the other between their lips. This is called a bunko and by the Portuguese a cheroota."

A later English sojourner to the Far East described "bunko" as "a little tobacco wrapt in the leaf of a tree, about the bigness of one's little finger." A Dutch botanist in Malaya found tobacco made into cigars by being wrapped in banana leaves. Another traveler noted cigars made with palm leaf as wrapper.

A major source of cigars in the Far East is the Philippines. Among the brands of handmades are Alhambra, Calixto Lopez, Flor de Manila, and Tabacalera. For Zino Davidoff, in pondering the type of cigar to be enjoyed, geography was just as important as time of day. Before lunch he found desirable a small cigar from the Philippines, Brazil, Jamaica, Mexico, the Canary Islands, the Netherlands, Belgium, or Germany. Thereafter, his senses deserved nothing less than a Havana. Should no Cuban be available, he would settle for the Flor de Isabela or Alhambra from the Philippines; Ornellas, La Prueba, or Costenos of Mexico; Jamaica's Tropical de Luxe; La Restina from Puerto Rico; from the Canary Islands a Don Miguel, Don Diego, or Flamenco; a Schimmelpennick of the Netherlands; E. Nobel or Hirschprung from Denmark; and Suerdick, Cruz de Almas, or the small Talvis from Brazil.

As for the United States, he wrote in *The Connoisseur's Book of the Cigar,* "It is necessary to admit that American cigars satisfy the taste of today's public for the light, refreshing cigar which can be smoked at any time or place without much effort." But, he warned, while it is true that all cigars finish in smoke, cigars are not the same "and it is not the same smoke."

The choice of cigar is a personal matter. Indeed, they seem to be available in as bewildering an array of colors, shapes, sizes, and national origins as those who smoke them. As in picking friends and lovers, there are no rules. In selecting it is, in the words of the song, "to each his own."

To My Cigar

The warmth of thy glow

Well-lighted cigar

Makes happy thoughts flow,

And drives sorrow afar.

Sweet cheer of sadness!

Life's own happy star!

I greet thee with gladness,

My friendly cigar!

—FRIEDRICH MARC

Lighting Up

A MAN'S SHOES WILL TELL YOU IF HE HAS MONEY, HIS
CLOTHES IF HE HAS STYLE. BUT IF YOU WANT TO KNOW IF
HE'S A SPORT, SEE IF HE'S WEARING A GOOD CIGAR.
—*Nat Sherman, tobacconist*

"A man falls in love with cigars the way he falls in love with a woman," said a student of the sociology of smoking. "He knows it immediately but explaining why he loves is not so easy to enunciate. We never really know what makes us fall in love. Should we want to? To know is to lift the veil of mystery."

Comparing the cigar with romance is most appropriate. The first time you smoke a cigar is like the first time you have sex. You have a pretty good idea what to do and you hope it will be as good as you've been told, but you're nervous and not sure how to get started.

The first decision is with whom to share the experience. In love, of course, this requires willingness on the part of someone else. The selection of a cigar is far more complex. First, it is done strictly solo. Second, the options present themselves in a bewildering array of shapes, sizes, colors, names, availability of packaging (singly or by the box), and range of price. The third factor that differentiates experiencing the world of cigars from the explorations of matters of the heart is that it is easier to recognize that a mistake has been made in one's choice of a cigar and then to move on—without the unpleasant consequences that can follow the ending of a love affair.

In smoking cigars, as in love, experience counts. The more you have, the more you learn and the better you become at it. As another writer put it, "The cigar smoker, like the perfect lover or the bagpipe player, is a calm man, slow and sure of his wind."

Cigar smoking engages all senses—sight, touch, smell, taste, and even hearing. Cigar maker Carlos Fuente Jr. places great emphasis on the look of the cigar's wrapper. It should be free of blemishes. Stains could be mildew. The wrapper must not appear to be coming undone. Plant ribs are not indicative of the best quality wrapper leaf. It should feel silky and smooth, elastic yet firm. Absence of cracks or ripples indicates that the cigar has been well humidified, ensuring that the smoke will be cool and, therefore, tastier. Gently rolled between thumb and index finger, it should be solid and not make a crackling sound. Soft spots mean the cigar has not been properly filled, and those gaps will burn unevenly and produce a hot, unpleasant draw.

"A quality cigar, well chosen and well preserved," Davidoff says, "ought to be free of unpleasant surprises."

As we explained earlier, the color of the wrapper is a guide to the cigar's flavor: light green (*Claro claro*) tastes slightly on the sweet side; *Claro* is light tan and neutral; brown to reddish brown *Colorado* has a rich and subtle aroma; Natural is light to brown and a bit stronger; English Market Selection (EMS) brings a slightly deeper shade of brown; *Maduro* (the Spanish for "ripe" or "mature") has a dark brown wrapper that should be silky and oily and offer a nut-sweet taste and mild aroma; and *Oscuro* is the darkest and strongest.

Regarding picking the appropriate shape, length, and thickness (ring gauge), the painter Van Dongen thought that the cigar ought to match the smoker's physique. But just as some short men feel perfectly comfortable with a taller woman, there are individuals who do not equate physiology with choice in cigars. New York City's Mayor Fiorello La Guardia was short and roly-poly but smoked long cigars, presumably because he felt the lengthier ones underscored his feisty and combative nature. Comedians who have employed cigars in their acts, such as Groucho Marx, W.C. Fields and George Burns, evidently decided that big ones contributed an even more antic atmosphere to their performances. Other men who picked large cigars in contrast to their body shapes and sizes seem to have done so in an effort to enhance their social, political, or economic status—or simply because they liked 'em big.

New York City's Mayor Fiorello LaGuardia was known as "the Little Flower," but he liked his cigars big. Courtesy of New York Public Library

The attraction of a cigar is in the eye, mind, heart, and soul of the individual. Indeed, a virtue of the cigar is that it can be as satisfying to the smoker with a cigarillo physique and a Churchill in his mouth as a demitasse in the hand of Arnold Schwarzenegger. But there is a caveat in switching between one size in a favorite brand to another of the same make. In their pamphlet "How to Judge a Good Cigar," Schielein and DiMeola point out that "the same cigar blends in different sizes taste different—sometimes vastly different—if there's a big difference in ring size and length."

Thus, if a maker excels in a cigar of 6½ inches with a 42 ring, it does not have to follow that the same brand in other sizes must be exactly like it and, therefore, equally satisfying. While a pipe smoker can feel certain that his favorite blend will taste the same if he buys it in one-ounce pouches or one-pound cans, the cigar smoker comes to learn that there can be big differences in what he gets in his preferred brand, depending upon the type of cigar chosen. Nor is there certainty in the brand names put on cigars by their makers.

As we have seen, many of the cigar artisans who fled Cuba in the 1960s took Cuban brand names with them, so that today the Punch brand, for example, comes from both Cuba and Honduras. Hoyo de Monterrey, Montecristo, Ramon Allones, Partagas, Fonseca, Por Laranaga, H. Upmann, and even La Gloria Cubana, which were originally Cuban, are now produced elsewhere. The only difference to be seen is the word "Habano" or "Havana" on the band. Whether a distinction can be recognized in taste has been a matter for debate for decades and is unlikely to be settled soon.

The origin of a cigar is often denoted on the packaging and the band. Those made in Cuba since 1985 carry a government stamp (Cubatabaco) and *Hecho en Cuba. Totalmente a Mano* ("Made in Cuba. Completely handmade") in black. *Hecho en Cuba* denotes a machine-made product. *Hecho a Mano* means the cigars are only partly hand-finished. Cuban brands available on the international market in 1995 were: Bolivar, Caney, Cifuentes, Cohiba, Diplomaticos, El Rey del Mundo, Fonseca, Gispert, H. Upmann, Hoyo de Monterrey, Jose L. Piedra, Juan Lopez, La

Corona, La Escepcion, La Flor de Cano, La Gloria Cubana, Montecristo, Partagas, Por Laranaga, Punch, Quai D'Orsay, Quintero y Hermanos, Rafael Gonzales, Ramon Allones, Romeo y Julieta, San Luis Rey, Sancho Panza, Siboney, Stantos de Luxe, and Troya.

Cuban cigars also carry a factory code in blue ink. These include JM (Jose Marti), FPG (Francisco Perez German), BM (Briones Montoto), FR (Fernando Roig) and EL (El Laguito). Non-Cuban boxes generally state the country of origin. American-produced cigars bear a code that begins with the letters TP. Some bands will also declare the vintage of the contents, which refers to the date of the crop harvest, not the year in which they were made. Many bands also announce the country of origin.

Some boxed cigars are also individually packaged in either cellophane or glass, plastic, wooden, or metal tubes. Other brands may come in ribbon-bound bundles. A few types are also packed in jars. (For information on the artistry and the collectibility of boxes and bands, see chapter 8)

In the more likely event that cigars are not bought by the box but are taken from the store one, two, or three at a time, it is the recommendation of the experts that they not be simply tucked unprotected in a pocket. The ideal way of carrying around cigars is in a holder. These are usually leather, metal, or plastic and accommodate two to four cigars. (For more on holders, see chapter 6)

Perhaps nothing in the entire universe of cigars can evoke a more heated debate than the issue of what to do about the band. Must it be removed before smoking or does it stay on? The debate is a relatively recent development in the history of cigars. Once upon a time the band served a practical purpose. It ensured that the wrapper did not come undone. Because today's technology has all but eliminated that unpleasantness, the role of a band is to identify the brand and often the country of origin of the cigar. Regardless of the practicalities of the cigar band, it has always been an integral part of the mystique of cigars and has become a highly desirable collectible.

Some who decry keeping the band on during smoking say that doing so is simply a means for the smoker to show off his discernment and excellent taste or, if the cigar is an expensive one, the wealth in his wallet. Detractors also insist that keeping a cigar band in place is a frightful demonstration of coarseness and ill breeding. In a scene in one of Sherlock Holmes's adventures on public television, the Sleuth of Baker Street (played by Jeremy Brett) advises the villain that if he persists in smoking cigars with the band on he will be "put down as a bounder."

On or off? To each his own!

No matter when and where a cigar is to be smoked, whether with band or without, the smoker must begin by making the cigar smokable. Because most premiums are rolled with a closed head, for the smoke to be drawn it has to be cut or punctured. Davidoff calls it "the decisive act." The smoker accomplishes this in one of three ways: using a cutting, clipping, or punching tool; pinching or tearing with the fingernails; or nipping with the teeth. Although there are aesthetic differences, the result will be effective: Smoke comes through. How much flows depends on the size of the opening. Ideally, it will be small, but always in proportion to the size of the cigar. The bigger the cigar, the greater the flow of smoke; therefore, the cut or opening should be larger. Some smokers wet the head in the mouth before making the cut.

The cigar is now primed for lighting. This would appear to be an easy act. But nothing concerning the cigar has ever been without controversy. For example, there are those who insist that prior to lighting, the entire cigar should be moistened. Others aver that its whole length should be warmed with a match, lighter, or candle. The latter practice once made sense. In the past, wrappers were customarily coated with a thin layer of special gum that, if not removed before smoking, added an unwelcome taste and odor to the smoke. Modern cigars are sealed with an odorless and tasteless vegetable gum. As to the warming of the exterior of the entire cigar, Zino Davidoff's book emphatically advises warming only the foot, very lightly.

How to light up? With a match? A lighter? For many years it was the tradition of cigar stores to keep a lighted candle or a gas-fed flame ready for the purpose. Ultra-purists in both cigar and pipe smoking swear by the wooden match. Invented in 1827, the pocket-sized boxes with sliding drawers of little sticks capped by a sulfur compound that burst into a flame with friction were commonplace by the 1850s. In the next decade modifications of the chemical makeup of the business end to prevent accidental flaming provided smokers with a "safety match." It would remain the primary means to light up until the arrival of petroleum-fueled mechanical lighters. One thing that those who still prefer matches have learned is that it is a good idea to have more than one match at hand for the purpose. Cigars, like pipes, can be cranky getting started, requiring more than one match.

Centuries of experience in lighting cigars results in these recommendations:

1. Hold the cigar tip horizontally and in direct contact with the flame, then slowly revolve it until you see the end is charred evenly over its entire surface.

2. Place the cigar between your lips, still keeping the body horizontal. Hold the flame about an inch away from the end and draw slowly as you turn it. Make sure it is evenly lit, otherwise one side will burn faster than the other.

3. Blow gently on the glowing end to ensure that it is burning evenly.

"Lighting is a serious and discreet act," Davidoff writes. "It is an act that requires care and excludes exhibitionism."

What about a cigar holder? Again, some use them. Those who do not feel as does Davidoff, who asks, "Who would want to drink a good wine with a straw?" As to the smoking, the bywords in Davidoff's book are adverbs: slowly, easily, nobly, peacefully, gracefully.

Auguste Barthelemy's tome, *L'art de fumer pipe et cigare*, decreed, "The true smoker abstains from imitating Vesuvius."

Cigar smoke is not inhaled. It is drawn into the mouth and held for several seconds. But it is not just the tongue that savors the smoke. Like a fine wine, a good cigar has "nose." The aroma is as important to one's enjoyment as is tantalizing the taste buds. And there is the smoke as it curls and eddies.

Francis Miles Finch wrote:

> *Floating away like the fountains' spray,*
> *Or the snow-white plume of a maiden,*
> *The smoke-wreaths rise to the starlit skies*
> *With blissful fragrance laden.*
> *Then smoke away till a golden ray*
> *Lights up the dawn of the morrow,*
> *For a cheerful cigar, like a shield will bar*
> *The blows of care and sorrow.*

Next, consider the ash as it lengthens. But do not treat it like the remnants of a cigarette, to be knocked away by rudely hitting it against the rim of an ashtray or flicking it off with a tap of the fingertip. Let it drop off naturally, either in a tray or in the palm of the hand: *never on the floor*.

How much of the cigar should be smoked? Your guide will be in the taste. The shorter it becomes, the harsher is the flavor. This is because of the concentration of tars. The pleasures of the taste are less when a cigar has burned halfway; in addition, it becomes difficult to keep it going. Beyond halfway, the concentration of tars will make it go out.

"A smoker of delicacy," Davidoff advises, "doesn't prolong it."

Let it go out by itself. Do not stamp it to death in an ashtray or squash it underfoot. Set it down gently and let it expire naturally. What to do with the remains? One point on which cigar lovers agree with nonsmokers is that a finished, cold cigar is not a pretty sight. Dispose of the remains as soon as you can. But do not mourn the loss. Dwell upon the pleasure it brought you, sniff the lingering traces of its glorious aroma in the air, and regard the fate of all good cigars as did one unknown poet:

> *Oh, their lives are sweet, but all too brief,*
> *And death doth their sweetness mar;*
> *But fragrance fine is forever thine,*
> *My well-beloved cigar!*

Besides, there's always the next one.

5

State
of the
Cigar

But after all I try in vain
To fetter my opinion;
Since each upon my giddy brain
Has boasted a dominion.
Comparisons, I'll not provoke
Lest all should be offended.
Let this discussion end in smoke
As many more have ended.

—HENRY S. LEIGH

The Constitution of the United States, Article II, Section Three, requires that the President of the United States "shall from time to time give to Congress Information on the State of the Union." Congress has not always agreed with the assessment. That's called politics.

What's judged best or true by one person may be deemed lacking in virtue or veracity by someone else.

Some people like caviar and debate which kind is supreme, while others shudder at the very notion of eating fish eggs.

Admirers of horses bet on different thoroughbreds, and that, as they say, "makes horse-races."

Subjectivity is human nature and contrary opinions are the essence of life's endless excitements.

So it has been and always will be with cigars. Therefore, in the expectation that voices will lift in ardent dissent, we herewith present our assessment of the current state of the world's cigars. The roster of cigar brands that we evaluated as worthy is presented in alphabetical order, beginning with the leading lights of the international trade, followed by a listing of brands made in the United States, accompanied by all pertinent data: nation of origin; style; length; ring; flavor/strength. A handy guide to judging strength of flavor is country of origin.

Brazil: on the heavy side, spicy
Cameroon: medium, spicy, and aromatic
Canary Islands: mild to medium
Cuba: medium to full bodied
Dominican Republic: generally mild
Ecuador: mild
Honduras: on the full-bodied and spicier side
Jamaica: somewhat lighter than Dominican
Mexico: highly variable from very mild to harsh
Nicaragua: medium and sweet
Philippines: mild
United States: mild

We intend our listings as guidelines to taste. They reflect our own assessment of quality and value, as well as a consensus of others who know their cigars. For purely subjective reasons, not all brands and styles are listed. And a few that are may be difficult to find. Our scale is the familiar classroom grading system. The very best get an A+, and so on through A, B, and C. Any brand that scored a D or F has been excluded.

RATINGS (INTERNATIONAL):

Brand/style /country	Size/ ring	Flavor	Grade
ADANTE (Dominican Republic)*			
No. 405			
Petit Corona	4½ x 42	Medium	B
No. 504			
Corona	5½ x 42	Medium	B
No. 603			
Palma Fina	6¼ x 34	Medium	B
No. 702			
Cetro	6 x 42	Medium	B
No. 801			
Elegante	6⅝ x 43	Medium	B
* No Longer made.			
AGUILA (Dominican Republic)			
Coronita	5½ x 40	Medium	B
Brevas 44	7½ x 44	Medium	B
Brevas 46	6½ x 46	Medium	B
Petit Gordo	4¾ x 50	Medium	B
ALHAMBRA (Philippines)			
Corona	5 x 42	Med–Full	C
Corona Grande	8¼ x 47	Med–Full	C
Double Corona	8½ x 50	Med–Full	C
Duque	6½ x 42	Med–Full	C
ANDUJAR (Dominican Republic)			
Azua	9 x 46	Med–Full	B
Macroix	6½ x 44	Medium	B
Romana	5 x 25	Medium	B
Samana	6 x 38	Medium	B
Santiago	7½ x 50	Medium	B

Brand/style /country	Size/ ring	Flavor	Grade
ALIADOS (Honduras)			
Churchill	7½ x 54	Full	B+
Corona Deluxe	6½ x 45	Med–Full	B
Figurin	10 x 60	Full	B
General	18 x 66	Full	B
Lonsdale	6½ x 42	Medium	B
Palma	7 x 36	Medium	B
Piramides	7½ x 60	Full	B
Remedios	5½ x 42	Medium	B
Rothschild	5 x 51	Medium	B
Toro	6 x 54	Med–Full	B
Valentino	7 x 48	Med–Full	B
#4 Extra	5½ x 45	Medium	B
ANTONIO & CLEOPATRA (Puerto Rico)			
Grenadier Corona	5½ x 44	Mild	B
Grenadier	6¼ x 33	Mild	B+
Grenadier Tubo	6 x 33	Mild	B+
Miniature Grenadier	4½ x 33	Mild	B
Panatela	5½ x 35	Mild	B
Sabers Plastic (hard to find)	6 x 30	Mild	C
Whiff	4½ x 26	Mild	B
ARANGO STATESMAN (Honduras)			
Barrister	7½ x 46	Med–Full	B
Counselor	5½ x 44	Med–Full	B
Executor	5 x 40	Med–Full	B

Brand/style /country	Size/ ring	Flavor	Grade
AROMAS de SAN ANDREAS (Mexico)			
Lonsdale Gourmet			
(tubed)	6¹/₂ x 42	Medium	B
ARTURO FUENTE (Dominican Republic)			
Brevas Royal	5¹/₂ x 42	Mild	A
Canone	8¹/₂ x 52	Medium	A
Chateau			
Fuente	4¹/₂ x 50	Medium	A
Churchill	7¹/₄ x 48	Full	A
Corona			
Imperial	6¹/₂ x 46	Medium	A
Cuban Corona	5¹/₄ x 45	Medium	A
Curly Head	6¹/₂ x 43	Medium	A
Curly Head			
Deluxe	6¹/₂ x 43	Medium	A
Dante	7 x 52	Medium	A
Double Chateau			
Fuente	6³/₄ x 50	Full	A
Flor Fina			
8-5-8	6 x 47	Medium	A
Fumas	7 x 44	Medium	A
Hemingway			
Classic	7 x 48	Medium	A
Hemingway			
Masterpiece	9 x 52	Full	A+
Hemingway			
Short Story	4 x 48	Mild	A+
Hemingway			
Signature	6 x 47	Medium	A
19-12	6¹/₄ x 42	Medium	A
Double			
Corona	7⁵/₈ x 46	Full	A
Panatela Fina	7 x 38	Medium	A
Petit Corona	5 x 38	Medium	A
Privada #1	6³/₄ x 44	Medium	A
Rothschild	4¹/₂ x 50	Medium	A
Royal Salute	7.62 x 54	Full	A
Spanish			
Lonsdale	6¹/₂ x 42	Medium	A

Brand/style /country	Size/ ring	Flavor	Grade
ASHTON (Dominican Republic)			
Aged Maduro			
#10	5 x 50	Full	A
#20	5¹/₂ x 44	Full	A
#30	6³/₄ x 44	Full	A
#40	6 x 50	Full	A
#50	7 x 48	Full	A
#60	7¹/₂ x 52	Full	A
Cabinet			
No. 1	9 x 52	Full	A
No. 2	7 x 46	Med–Full	A
No. 3	6 x 46	Med–Full	A
Churchill	7¹/₂ x 52	Medium	A
Cordial	5 x 30	Mild	A
Corona	5¹/₂ x 44	Mild	A
8-9-8	6¹/₂ x 44	Mild	A
Elegante	6¹/₂ x 35	Mild	A
Magnum	5 x 50	Medium	A
No. 20			
Maduro	5¹/₂ x 44	Medium	A
No. 30			
Maduro	6³/₄ x 44	Medium	A
No. 50			
Maduro	7¹/₂ x 52	Med–Full	A
No. 60			
Maduro	7¹/₂ x 52	Med–Full	A
Panatela	6 x 36	Mild	A
Prime Minister	6⁷/₈ x 48	Medium	A
ASTRAL (Honduras)			
Beso	5 x 52	Full	B+
Favorito	7 x 48	Full	B+
Lujo	6¹/₂		
	x 44	Full	B+
Maestro	7¹/₂		
	x 52	Full	B+
Perfeccion	7 x 48	Full	B+
AVO (Dominican Republic)			
No. 1	6³/₄ x 42	Mild	A
No. 2	6 x 50	Medium	A

Brand/style /country	Size/ ring	Flavor	Grade
No. 3	7¹/₂ x 52	Medium	A
No. 4	7 x 38	Mild	A
No. 6	6¹/₂ x 36	Mild	A
No. 7	6 x 44	Mild	A
No. 8	5¹/₂ x 40	Mild	A
No. 9	4³/₄ x 48	Medium	A
Belicoso	6 x 50	Medium	A
Especiales	8 x 48	Medium	A
Intermezzo	5¹/₂ x 50	Medium	A
Maestoso	7 x 48	Medium	A
Petit Belicoso	4³/₄ x 50	Medium	A
Preludio	6 x 40	Medium	A
Pyramid	7 x 54	Medium	A

BACCARAT (Honduras)

Bonitas	4¹/₂ x 30	Mild	B
Churchill	7 x 50	Med–Full	B
Havana Twist	7 x 44	Medium	B
Luchadore	6 x 44	Medium	B
No. 1	7 x 43	Medium	B
No. 2	6¹/₄ x 43	Medium	B
No. 4	5¹/₂ x 42	Medium	B
Palma Fina	7 x 36	Medium	B
Petit Corona	5¹/₂ x 42	Medium	B
Platinum	4¹/₂ x 32	Mild	B
Repeater 100	5¹/₂ x 44	Medium	B
200	6 x 44	Medium	B
300	6¹/₂ x 44	Medium	B
Rothschild	5 x 50	Full	B

BANCES (Honduras)

Breva	5¹/₄ x 43	Medium	B
Cazadore	6¹/₄ x 44	Medium	B
Corona Immensas	6³/₄ x 48	Medium	B+
Demitasse	4 x 35	Mild	B
El Prado	6.12 x 36	Medium	B
Havana Holder	6¹/₂ x 30	Medium	B
Palma	6 x 42	Medium	B
Unique	5¹/₂ x 38	Mild	B

BAUZA (Dominican Republic)

Casa Grande	6³/₄ x 48	Medium	B

Brand/style /country	Size/ ring	Flavor	Grade
Fabuloso	7¹/₂ x 50	Med–Full	B
Florete	6⁷/₈ x 35	Medium	B
Grecos	5¹/₂ x 42	Medium	B
Jaguar	6¹/₂ x 42	Medium	B
Medaglia d'Oro	6⁷/₈ x 44	Medium	B
Petit Corona	5 x 38	Medium	B
Presidente	7¹/₂ x 50	Med–Full	B+
Robusto	5¹/₂ x 50	Medium	B

BELINDA (Honduras)

Brevas Conserva	5¹/₂ x 43	Mild	B
Cabinet	5¹/₂ x 45	Mild	B
Corona Grande	6¹/₄ x 44	Medium	B
Medaglia d'Oro	4¹/₂ x 50	Medium	B
Ramon	7¹/₄ x 47	Medium	B

BERING (Honduras)

Baron	7¹/₄ x 42	Medium	B
Casino	7¹/₈ x 42	Medium	B
Cazadore	6¹/₄ x 45	Medium	B
Corona Grande	6¹/₄ x 46	Medium	B
Corona Royal	6 x 41	Medium	B
Coronado	5¹/₄ x 44	Medium	B
Eights	4¹/₄ x 32	Mild	B
Gold #1	6¹/₄ x 33	Mild	B
Hispano	6 x 50	Medium	B
Immensa	7¹/₈ x 45	Medium	B
Imperial	5¹/₄ x 42	Medium	B
Plaza	6 x 43	Medium	B

BERMEJO (Honduras)

Cazadores	6¹/₄ x 46	Med–Full	B-
Fumas	6¹/₂ x 45	Med–Full	B-

BEVERLY HILLS (Honduras)

No. 535	5 x 35	Medium	B
No. 550	5 x 50	Medium	B
No. 644	6 x 44	Medium	B
No. 736	7 x 36	Medium	B
No. 749	7 x 49	Medium	B

Brand/style /country	Size/ ring	Flavor	Grade
BLUE RIBBON (Honduras)			
No. 500	7¹/₂ x 52	Medium	B
No. 501	6 x 50	Medium	B
No. 502	4³/₄ x 50	Medium	B
No. 503	6¹/₂ x 44	Medium	B
No. 504	5¹/₂ x 42	Medium	B
BOHEMIA (Dominican Republic)			
Cuban Twist	5 x 42	Mild	B
BOLIVAR (Cuba)			
Belicosos Finos	5¹/₄ x 52	Full	A
Bonitas	5 x 40	Full	A
Corona	5⁵/₈ x 42	Full	A
Corona Extra	5⁵/₈ x 44	Full	A
Corona Gigantes/ Churchill	7 x 47	Full	A
Corona Junior	4⁵/₁₆ x 42	Full	A
Gold Medal/ Lonsdale	6¹/₂ x 42	Full	A
Petit Corona	5 x 42	Full	A
Palmas (Panatela)	7 x 33	Full	A
Royal Corona (Robusto)	4⁷/₈ x 50	Full	A
BOLIVAR (Dominican Republic)			
Belicoso Fino	6¹/₂ x 38	Mild	A
Bolivares	7 x 46	Medium	A
Corona Extra	5¹/₂ x 42	Mild	A
Corona Grand	6¹/₂ x 42	Medium	A
Panatelita	6 x 38	Mild	A-
BUTERA ROYAL VINTAGE (Dominican Republic)			
Bravo Corto	4¹/₂ x 50	Medium	B
Capo Grande (Churchill)	7¹/₂ x 48	Medium	B
Cedro Fino	6¹/₂ x 44	Medium	B
Dorado 652 (Toro)	6 x 52	Medium	B

Brand/style /country	Size/ ring	Flavor	Grade
CABALLEROS (Dominican Republic)			
Churchill	7 x 50	Medium	B
Corona	5³/₄ x 43	Medium	B
Double Corona	6³/₄ x 48	Medium	B
Petit Corona	5¹/₂ x 42	Medium	B
Rothschild	5 x 50	Medium	B
CABANAS (Dominican Republic)			
Corona	5¹/₂ x 42	Mild	B
Exquisito	6¹/₂ x 48	Med–Full	B
Premier	6⁵/₈ x 42	Medium	B
Royale	5⁵/₈ x 46	Medium	B
CALIXTO LOPEZ (Philippines)			
Corona Exquisito	5³/₈ x 43	Mild	B
Czar	8 x 45	Medium	B
Gigantes	8¹/₂ x 50	Medium	B
Lonsdale	6³/₄ x 42	Medium	B
Nobles	6¹/₂ x 50	Medium	B
No. 1	6³/₈ x 45	Medium	B
CAMACHO (Honduras)			
#1	7 x 44	Medium	B
Churchill	7 x 44	Medium	B
Monarca	5 x 50	Medium	B
Nacionales	5¹/₂ x 44	Medium	B
Palma	6 x 43	Medium	B
CANARIA d'ORO (Dominican Republic)			
Babies	4¹/₄ x 32	Mild	A
Corona	5¹/₂ x 42	Medium	A
Fino	6 x 31	Mild	A
Immensos	5¹/₂ x 49	Medium	A
Lonsdale	6¹/₂ x 42	Medium	A
Rothschild	4¹/₂ x 50	Medium	A
Vista (no longer made)	6¹/₄ x 32	Mild	A
CARRINGTON (Dominican Republic)			
#1	7¹/₂ x 50	Full	B
#2	6 x 43	Medium	B

Brand/style /country	Size/ ring	Flavor	Grade
#5	6⁷/₈ x 46	Medium	B
#6	4³/₄ x 50	Medium	B
#7	6 x 50	Medium	B
CASA BLANCA (Dominican Republic)			
Bonitas	4 x 36	Mild	B
Corona	5¹/₂ x 42	Mild	B
De Luxe	6 x 50	Mild	B
Half Jeroboam	5 x 66	Mild	B
Lonsdale	6¹/₂ x 42	Mild	B+
Magnum	7 x 60	Mild–Med	B
Panatela	6 x 35	Mild	B
Presidente	7¹/₂ x 50	Mild–Med	B
CASA de NICARAGUA (Nicaragua)			
Churchill	7 x 49	Medium	C+
Corona	5¹/₂ x 42	Medium	C
Double Corona Lonsdale	7 x 44	Medium	C
CASA MARTIN (Dominican Republic)			
Churchill	6⁷/₈ x 46	Medium	B
Majestad	7¹/₂ x 50	Medium	B
Matador	6 x 50	Medium	B
CENTENNIAL "V" (Honduras)			
Cetros	6¹/₄ x 44	Medium	B
Churchill	7 x 48	Full	B
Corona	5¹/₂ x 42	Medium	B
Presidente	8 x 50	Full	B
Robusto	5 x 50	Med–Full	B
Torpedo	7 x 36/54	Med–Full	B
#2	6 x 50	Medium	B
CERVANTES (Honduras)			
Churchill	7¹/₄ x 45	Medium	B
Corona	6¹/₄ x 42	Medium	B
Senadores	6 x 42	Medium	B
CHEVERE (Jamaica)			
Kingston	7 x 49	Medium	B
Montega	6¹/₂ x 45	Medium	B
Ochos Rios	8 x 49	Med–Full	B
Port Antonio	5¹/₂ x 43	Medium	B
Spanish Town	6¹/₂ x 42	Medium	B

Brand/style /country	Size/ ring	Flavor	Grade
CIBAO (Dominican Republic)			
Brevas	5¹/₄ x 50	Medium	A-
Churchill	6³/₄ x 46	Medium	A
Corona Deluxe	5¹/₂ x 43	Medium	A
Diamantes	6¹/₂ x 35	Medium	A
Elegantes	7 x 44	Medium	A
COHIBA (Cuba)			
Coronas Especial	6 x 38	Medium	A+
Esplendido/ Churchill	7 x 47	Full	A+
Exquisito	5 x 36	Medium	A+
Lancero	7¹/₂ x 38	Medium	A+
Panatela	4¹/₂ x 26	Medium	A+
Robusto	5 x 36	Medium	A+
Siglo I	4 x 40	Medium	A+
II	5 x 42	Medium	A+
III	6 x 42	Medium	A+
IV	5⁵/₈ x 46	Med–Full	A+
V	6³/₄ x 43	Medium	A+
COHIBA (Dominican Republic)			
Corona Especiale	6¹/₂ x 43	Mild	A-
Esplendido	7 x 49	Mild	A-
Robusto	5¹/₂ x 50	Mild	A-
CONDAL (Canary Islands)			
No. 1 Lonsdale	6⁵/₈ x 42	Mild	B
No. 3 Corona	5⁵/₈ x 42	Mild	B
No. 4 Corona	5¹/₄ x 42	Mild	B
No. 6 Panatela	6¹/₄ x 35	Mild	B
Immenso	7¹/₄ x 42	Mild	B
CORTESIA (Honduras)			
#1	5¹/₂ x 40	Mild	B
#2	5¹/₄ X 44	Mild	B
#5	6¹/₄ x 44	Medium	B
#6	6³/₄ x 48	Medium	B
#7	7¹/₄ x 52	Med–Full	B

Brand/style /country	Size/ ring	Flavor	Grade
CREDO (Dominican Republic)			
Anthanore	5³/₄ x 42	Mild	B
Arcane	5 x 50	Medium	B
Jubilate	5 x 34	Mild	B
Magnificat	6⁷/₈ x 46	Medium	B
Pythagoras	7 x 50	Full	B
CRUZ REAL (Mexico)			
No. 1 Lonsdale	6⁵/₈ x 42	Medium	B-
No. 19 Toro	6 x 50	Medium	B-
No. 25 Robusto	5¹/₂ x 50	Medium	B-
CUBITA (Dominican Republic)			
#2	6¹/₄ x 38	Medium	B
#500	5¹/₂ x 43	Medium	B-
#700	6 x 50	Medium	B-
#2000	7 x 50	Medium	B
8-9-8	6³/₄ x 43	Medium	B
CUESTA REY (Dominican Republic/Tampa)			
Caravelle	6¹/₄ x 34	Mild	B
Captiva	6³/₁₆ x 42	Mild	B
Dominican #1	8¹/₂ x 52	Full	B
#2	7¹/₄ x 48	Medium	B
#3	7 x 36	Medium	B
#4	6¹/₂ x 42	Medium	B
#5	5¹/₂ x 43	Mild	B
1884	6¹/₂ x 44	Mild	B
No. 95	6¹/₄ x 42	Mild	B
No. 898	7 x 49	Medium	B
SPECIAL CARIBBEANS (Dominican Republic)			
Churchill	7 x 48	Medium	B
Corona	5¹/₂ x 43	Medium	B
Fino	6 x 35	Medium	B
No. 1	6³/₄ x 43	Medium	B
No. 2	6.37 x 42	Medium	B
No. 898	6¹/₂ x 45	Medium	B

Brand/style /country	Size/ ring	Flavor	Grade
Nom Plus	5¹/₂ x 50	Medium	B
Port au Prince	7.62 x 52	Medium	
DAVIDOFF (Cuba)*			
Ambassadrice	4¹/₂ x 26	Mild	A+
Chateau Haut Brion	4 x 40	Mild	A+
Chateau Lafitte-Rothschild	4¹/₂ x 42	Mild	A+
Chateau Latour (corona)	5¹/₂ x 42	Mild	A+
Chateau Margaux	5 x 42	Mild	A+
Chateau Mouton-Rothschild	6 x 42	Medium	A+
Davidoff No. 1	7¹/₂ x 38	Medium	A+
Davidoff No. 2	6 x 38	Mild	A+
Davidoff 1000	4⁵/₈ x 34	Mild	A+
2000	5 x 42	Mild	A+
3000	7 x 33	Medium	A+
4000	6 x 42	Medium	A+
5000 (corona gorda)	5⁵/₈ x 46	Medium	A+
Dom Perignon (Churchill)	7 x 47	Medium	A+

Manufacturer discontinued production in Cuba. Some Cuban Davidoffs are still available.

Brand/style /country	Size/ ring	Flavor	Grade
DAVIDOFF (Dominican Republic)			
Ambassadrice	4⁵/₈ x 26	Mild	A
Anniversario No. 1	8¹¹/₁₆ x 48	Medium	A
Anniversario No. 2	7 x 48	Medium	A
Davidoff 1000	4⁵/₈ x 34	Mild	A
2000	5 x 42	Mild	A
3000	7 x 33	Medium	A
4000	6¹/₂ x 42	Mild	A
5000	5⁵/₈ x 42	Mild	A

Brand/style /country	Size/ ring	Flavor	Grade
Grand Cruz			
No. 1	6¹/₈ x 42	Medium	A
2	5⁵/₈ x 42	Medium	A
3	5 x 42	Mild	A
4	4⁵/₈ x 40	Mild	A
5	4 x 40	Mild	A
DIANA SILVIUS (Dominican Republic)			
Churchill	7 x 50	Med–Full	B
Corona	6¹/₂ x 42	Medium	B
Robusto	4⁷/₈ x 52	Medium	B
DIPLOMATICOS (Cuba)			
No.			
1 (Lonsdale)	6¹/₂ x 42	Medium	A+
2 (Torpedo)	6¹/₈ x 52	Med–Full	A+
3 (Corona)	5¹/₂ x 42	Medium	A+
4	5 x 42	Medium	A+
5	4 x 40	Medium	A+
6 (Especial)	7¹/₂ x 38	Medium	A+
7	6 x 38	Medium	A+
DON ASA (Honduras)			
Blunts	5 x 42	Medium	B+
Cetros	6¹/₂ x 44	Medium	B+
Coronas	5¹/₂ x 50	Full	B+
Imperial	8 x 44	Medium	B+
President	7¹/₂ x 50	Full	B+
Rothchild	4¹/₂ x 50	Full	B+
DON DIEGO (Dominican Republic)			
Babies	5.12 x 33	Mild	A
Corona	5.62 x 42	Mild	A
Corona Major	5.1 x 42	Mild	A
Grandes	6 x 50	Medium	A
Greco	6.5 x 38	Medium	A
Imperial	7.35 x 46	Medium	A
Lonsdale	6.62 x 42	Medium	A
Monarch	7¹/₄ x 46	Medium	A
Petit Corona	5.12 x 42	Mild	A
Prelude	4 x 28	Mild	A
Privada Chico*	5 x 33	Mild	A
No. 1*	6.75 x 43	Medium	A
2*	6.62 x 42	Medium	A
3*	6.62 x 38	Medium	A
4*	5.75 x 42	Medium	A

*Sold through catalogs.

Brand/style /country	Size/ ring	Flavor	Grade
DON JUAN (Nicaragua)			
Lindas	5¹/₂ x 38	Medium	C
Matador	6 x 50	Medium	C
Palma Fina	6⁷/₈ x 36	Medium	C
DON LEO (Dominican Republic)			
Cetro	6¹/₂ x 44	Medium	A-
Churchill	7¹/₂ x 50	Full	A-
Corona	5¹/₂ x 42	Medium	A-
Robusto	4¹/₂ x 50	Full	A-
Toro	6 x 50	Full	A-
DON LINO (Honduras)			
Churchill	7¹/₂ x 50	Med–Full	B
Corona	5¹/₂ x 50	Med–Full	B
#1	6¹/₂ x 44	Medium	B
#4	5 x 42	Medium	B
DON LINO HAVANA RESERVES (Honduras)			
Churchill	7¹/₂ x 50	Med–Full	B
Panatela	7 x 36	Medium	B
Robusto	5¹/₂ x 50	Medium	B
Toros	5¹/₂ x 46	Medium	B
#1	6¹/₂ x 44	Medium	B
DON MATEO (Honduras)			
No. 1	7 x 30	Medium	B
No. 2	6⁷/₈ x 35	Medium	B
No. 3	6 x 42	Medium	B
No. 4	5¹/₂ x 44	Medium	B
No. 5	6⁵/₈ x 44	Medium	B
No. 6	6⁷/₈ x 48	Medium	B
No. 7	4³/₄ x 50	Medium	B
No. 8	6¹/₄ x 50	Med–Full	B
No. 9	7¹/₂ x 50	Full	B
No. 10	8 x 52	Full	B

Brand/style /country	Size/ ring	Flavor	Grade
DON RAMOS (Honduras)			
Corona	$5^1/_2$ x 42	Medium	A
Especial	$6^7/_8$ x 36	Medium	A
Gigantes	$6^3/_4$ x 47	Medium	A
Gordas	$4^1/_2$ x 50	Medium	A
Magnum	$6^1/_4$ x 44	Med–Full	A
Petit Corona	5 x 42	Medium	A
Tres Petit Corona	4 x 42	Medium	A
DON TOMAS (Honduras)			
Blunt	5 x 42	Medium	A
Cetro No. 2	$6^1/_2$ x 44	Med–Full	A
Corona Grande	$6^1/_2$ x 44	Med–Full	A
Gigante	$8^1/_2$ x 52	Full	A
Imperial	8 x 44	Full	A
Panatela	6 x 36	Med–Full	A
Panatela Larga	7 x 36	Full	A
President	$7^1/_2$ x 50	Full	A
Rothschild	$4^1/_2$ x 50	Med–Full	A
Supremo	$6^1/_4$ x 42	Med–Full	A
Toro	$5^5/_8$ x 46	Medium	A
DUNHILL (Canary Islands)			
Corona	$5^1/_2$ x 43	Medium	A+
Corona Extra	$5^1/_2$ x 50	Medium	A+
Corona Grande	$6^1/_2$ x 43	Medium	A+
Lonsdale Grande	$7^1/_2$ x 42	Medium	A+
Panatela	6 x 30	Medium	A+
DUNHILL (Dominican Republic)			
Altamiras (tube)	5 x 48	Med–Full	A+
Cabreras (tube)	7 x 48	Med–Full	A+
Centenas (pyramid)	6 x 50	Med–Full	A+
Condados (Corona extra)	6 x 48	Med–Full	A+
Diamantes	$6^5/_8$ x 42	Med–Full	A+
Fantinos	7 x 28	Medium	A+
Peravias	7 x 50	Full	A+
Romanas	$4^1/_2$ x 50	Med–Full	A+
Tabaras	$5^9/_{16}$ x 42	Med–Full	A+
Valverdes	$5^9/_{16}$ x 42	Medium	A+
EL BESO (Mexico)			
Churchill	$7^1/_2$ x 50	Medium	C+
Toro	6 x 50	Medium	C+
EL POTOSI (Honduras)			
Corona	6.12 x 46	Medium	B-
Plaza	5.88 x 43	Medium	B-
EL REY del MUNDO (Honduras)			
Cafe au Lait	$4^1/_2$ x 35	Medium	A
Cedars	7 x 54	Medium	A
Choix Supreme	5 x 48	Medium	A
Coronas De Luxe	$5^1/_2$ x 42	Medium	A
Demitasse	4 x 30	Mild	A
Elegante	$5^3/_8$ x 29	Medium	A
Flor de Llaneza (pyramid)	$6^1/_2$ x 54	Med–Full	A
Flor del Mundo	$7^1/_4$ x 54	Med–Full	A
Gran Corona	$5^1/_2$ x 46	Medium	A
Isabel	$5^1/_2$ x 43	Medium	A
Lonsdale	$6^1/_2$ x 42	Medium	A
Petit Corona	5 x 42	Medium	A
Petit Lonsdale	$4^3/_4$ x 43	Medium	A
Rectangulares	$5^5/_8$ x 45	Medium	A
Reynitas	5 x 38	Medium	A
Robusto	5 x 54	Med–Full	A
Robusto Largo	6 x 54	Med–Full	A
Robusto Suprema	$7^1/_4$ x 54	Med–Full	A
Robusto Zavalla	5 x 54	Medium	A
Rothschild	5 x 50	Med–Full	A
Tainos (Churchill)	7 x 47	Med–Full	A
EVELIO (Honduras)			
Corona	$5^3/_4$ x 42	Medium	B+
Double Corona	$7^5/_8$ x 47	Medium	B+
#1	7 x 44	Medium	B+

Brand/style /country	Size/ ring	Flavor	Grade
Robusto	4³/₄ x 54	Full	B+
Robusto Larga	6 x 54	Full	B+
Torpedo	7 x 36/54	Full	B+

EXCALIBUR (Honduras)

Brand/style	Size/ring	Flavor	Grade
No. I	7¹/₄ x 54	Full	A
No. II	6³/₄ x 47	Med–Full	A
No. III	6¹/₈ x 50	Med–Full	A
No. IV	5⁵/₈ x 45	Med–Full	A
No. V	6¹/₈ x 44	Med–Full	A
No. VI	5³/₈ x 38	Medium	A
No. VII	5 x 43	Medium	A

FONSECA (Dominican Republic)

Brand/style	Size/ring	Flavor	Grade
Triangular	5¹/₂ x 56	Medium	B
#2-2	4¹/₄ x 40	Mild	B
#5-50	5 x 50	Medium	B
#7-9-9	6¹/₂ x 46	Medium	B
#8-9-8	6 x 43	Medium	B
#10-10	7 x 50	Full	B

GISPERT (Cuba)

Brand/style	Size/ring	Flavor	Grade
Corona	5⁵/₈ x 42	Mild	A
Habaneras #2	4⁵/₈ x 35	Mild	A
Petit Corona De Luxe	5 x 42	Mild	A

GRIFFIN'S (Dominican Republic)

Brand/style	Size/ring	Flavor	Grade
Don Bernardo	9 x 46	Mild/Sweet	A+
Griffinos	3³/₄ x 18	Mild/Sweet	A+
Prestige	7¹/₂ x 50	Mild/Sweet	A+
Privilege	5 x 30	Mild/Sweet	A+
No. 100	7 x 38	Mild/Sweet	A+
200	7 x 44	Mild/Sweet	A+
300	6¹/₄ x 44	Mild/Sweet	A+
400	6 x 38	Mild/Sweet	A+

HARROWS (Philippines)

Brand/style	Size/ring	Flavor	Grade
Camelot	7 x 43	Medium	C
Esquire	6 x 33	Mild	C
Londonderry	8 x 48	Medium	C
No. 1	6¹/₄ x 43	Medium	C
Regent	5⁵/₈ x 44	Mild	C

HENRY CLAY (Dominican Republic)

Brand/style	Size/ring	Flavor	Grade
Brevas	5¹/₂ x 42	Medium	B
Brevas Conserva	5⁵/₈ x 46	Medium	B
Brevas Fina	6¹/2 x 48	Medium	B

HENRY WINTERMANNS (Holland)

Brand/style	Size/ring	Flavor	Grade
Cafe Creme	2.88 x 28	Mild	A
Cafe Noir	2.88 x 28	Mild	A
Senorita	4 x 32	Mild	A
Slim Panatela	6 x 26	MIld	A

HIDALGO (Panama)

Brand/style	Size/ring	Flavor	Grade
Cazadore	7 x 44	Medium	C
Corona	5¹/₂ x 42	Medium	C
Monarch	8¹/₂ x 52	Medium	C

HINDS BROTHERS (Honduras)

Hand rolled in the Danlí valley, the Honduran selection consists of Honduran long-leaf filler and double binder and a rich, slightly spicy Equadorian leaf.

Brand/style	Size/ring	Flavor	Grade
Churchill	7 x 49	Med–Full	A
Corona	5¹/₂ x 42	Med–Full	A
President	8¹/₂ x 52	Full	A+
Robusto	5 x 50	Full	A+
Royal Corona	6 x 43	Med–Full	A
Short Churchill	6 x 50	Med–Full	A
Supremo	7 x 43	Med–Full	A
Torpedo	6 x 36/52	Med–Full	A

HINDS BROTHERS (Nicaragua)

Introduced in 1995, available in EMS and Maduro.

Brand/style	Size/ring	Flavor	Grade
Churchill	7 x 49	Med–Full	A
Corona	5¹/₂ x 42	Med–Full	A
Lonsdale Extra	7 x 43	Med–Full	A
Robusto	5 x 50	Med–Full	A
Short Churchill	6 x 50	Med–Full	A
Torpedo	6 x 52	Med–Full	A

Brand/style /country	Size/ ring	Flavor	Grade
HOLT'S (Honduras)*			
Connoisseur			
#1	6¹/₈ x 50	Medium	B
#2	6¹/₄ x 44	Medium	B
#3	6⁷/₈ x 48	Medium	B
#4	5 x 50	Medium	B
#5	7¹/₄ x 52	Medium	B
Natural Supremes			
#100	7¹/₄ x 54	Medium	B
#200	6¹/₄ x 44	Medium	B
#300	5¹/₂ x 45	Medium	B
#400	5¹/₂ x 44	Medium	B
#500	6¹/₂ x 43	Medium	B
Pyramid	7¹/₂ x 31–60	Medium	B
Torpedo	7¹/₂ x 31–60	Medium	B
Special Maduro			
Chairman	7¹/₂ x 52	Med–Full	B
Churchill	7 x 50	Med–Full	B
Presidente	8¹/₂ x 52	Med–Full	B
Rothschild	4¹/₂ x 50	Med–Full	B
Toro	6 x 50	Med–Full	B
#1	6³/₄ x 50	Med–Full	B
#4	5¹/₂ x 43	Med–Full	B

* *Sold through catalogs.*

Brand/style /country	Size/ ring	Flavor	Grade
HOYO de MONTERREY (Cuba)			
Churchill	7 x 47	Mild	A+
Corona	5¹/₂ x 42	Mild	A+
Double Corona	5¹/₂ x 42	Mild	A+
Epicure No. 1	5⁵/₈ x 46	Mild	A+
Epicure No. 2	4⁷/₈ x 50	Mild	A+
Jeanne d'Arc	5⁵/₈ x 35	Mild	A+
Le Hoyo du Dieux	6¹/₈ x 42	Mild	A+
Le Hoyo du Prince	5 x 40	Mild	A+
Le Hoyo du Roi	5¹/₂ x 42	Mild	A+
Margarita	4³/₄ x 26	Mild	A+

Brand/style /country	Size/ ring	Flavor	Grade
HOYO de MONTERREY (Honduras)			
Ambassador	6¹/₈ x 44	Medium	B
Cafe Royal	5¹/₄ x 44	Medium	B
Churchill	6¹/₄ x 45	Medium	B
Corona	5⁵/₈ x 46	Medium	B
Cuban Largo	7¹/₈ x 47	Med–Full	B+
Culebra	6¹/₄ x 35	Medium	B
Demi-Tasse	4 x 39	Mild	B
Double Corona	6³/₄ x 48	Medium	B
Excellente (no longer made)	6¹/₂ x 42	Medium	B
Falcon (no longer made)	6¹/₂ x 34	Medium	B
Governor	6¹/₂ x 50	Med–Full	B
Largos Elegante	7¹/₄ x 34	Med–Full	B
Margarita	5¹/₄ x 29	Medium	B
Petit Cetto	5¹/₂ x 42	Medium	B
President	8¹/₂ x 50	Full	B
Rothschild	4¹/₂ x 52	Medium	B
Sabrassos	5 x 40	Medium	B
Solitaire	6 x 50	Medium	B
Starbrite	4¹/₂ x 50	Medium	B
Super Hoyo	5¹/₂ x 44	Medium	B
Sultan	7¹/₄ x 54	Full	B+
#1	6¹/₂ x 43	Medium	B
#55	5¹/₄ x 43	Mefdium	B

Brand/style /country	Size/ ring	Flavor	Grade
H. UPMANN (Cuba)			
Churchill (also called Sir Winston)	7 x 47	Medium	A+
Connoisseur No. 1 (Robusto)	5 x 48	Mild	A+
Corona	5¹/₂ x 42	Mild	A+
Corona Junior	4¹/₂ x 36	Mild	A+
Corona Major	5¹/₈ x 42	Mild	A+
Grand Corona	5³/₄ x 40	Mild	A+
Lonsdale	6¹/₂ x 42	Medium	A+
Magnum	5¹/₂ x 46	Medium	A+
Monarcas	7 x 47	Medium	A+

Brand/style /country	Size/ ring	Flavor	Grade
Petit Corona	5 x 42	Mild	A+
Petit Upmann	4^{1}/$_{2}$ x 36	Mild	A+
Royal Corona	5^{1}/$_{2}$ x 42	Mild	A+
Super Corona	5^{1}/$_{2}$ x 46	Mild	A+
Upmann No. 2 (torpedo)	6^{1}/$_{2}$ x 42	Medium	A+

H. UPMANN (Dominican Republic)

Brand/style	Size/ring	Flavor	Grade
After Dinner	5.62 x 46	Medium	A
Amatista	5^{7}/$_{8}$ x 42	Medium	A
Aperitif	4 x 28	Mild	A
Churchill	5^{5}/$_{8}$ x 46	Medium	A
Columbo	8 x 50	Med–Full	A
Cordiale	4^{1}/$_{2}$ x 42	Medium	A
Corona Brava	6^{1}/$_{2}$ x 48	Medium	A
Corona Cristales	5^{9}/$_{16}$ x 42	Medium	A
Corona Imperiales	7 x 46	Med–Full	A
Corona Major	5.12 x 42	Medium	A
Corsarios	5 x 50	Medium	A
Crown Imperial	7.12 x 45	Med–Full	A
Demi-Tasse	4^{1}/$_{2}$ x 33	Mild	A
El Prado	7 x 36	Medium	A
Emperadore	7^{3}/$_{4}$ x 46	Medium	A
Extra Fino	6^{3}/$_{4}$ x 38	Medium	A
Fino	6.12 x 36	Medium	A
Lonsdale	6^{5}/$_{8}$ x 42	Medium	A
Monarch	7 x 46	Medium	A
Naturale	6.12 x 36	Medium	A
New Yorker	5.62 x 42	Medium	A
Panatela Cristales	6^{3}/$_{4}$ x 38	Medium	A
Pequenoes #100	4^{1}/$_{2}$ x 50	Medium	A
#200	4^{1}/$_{2}$ x 46	Medium	A
#300	4^{1}/$_{2}$ x 42	Medium	A
Petit Corona	5^{1}/$_{6}$ x 42	Medium	A
Robusto	4^{3}/$_{4}$ x 50	Medium	A
Rothschild	4^{1}/$_{2}$ x 50	Medium	A
#2000	7 x 42	Medium	A

JAMAICA BAY (Jamaica)*

Brand/style	Size/ring	Flavor	Grade
No. 100 Double Corona	7^{1}/$_{2}$ x 49	Med–Full	B+
No. 300 Lonsdale	6^{3}/$_{4}$ x 45	Med–Full	B+
No. 500 Panatela	6^{3}/$_{4}$ x 38	Med–Full	B+

* Sold through catalogs.

JAMAICAN GOLD (Jamaica)

Brand/style	Size/ring	Flavor	Grade
Baron	6^{1}/$_{2}$ x 44	Med–Full	B+
Count	5^{1}/$_{2}$ x 38	Med–Full	B+
Duke	5^{1}/$_{2}$ x 42	Med–Full	B+
Duchess	4^{1}/$_{2}$ x 30	Med–Full	B+
Earl	6^{3}/$_{4}$ x 38	Med–Full	B+
King	6 x 50	Med–Full	B+

JAMAICAN KINGS (Jamaica)*

Brand/style	Size/ring	Flavor	Grade
Buccaneer	6 x 42	Med–Full	B+
Governor	6 x 50	Med–Full	B+
Imperial	7^{1}/$_{2}$ x 50	Med–Full	B+
Prince	7^{3}/$_{4}$ x 50	Medium	B+
Rapier	7 x 36	Med–Full	B+

* Sold through catalogs.

JAMAICAN SUPREME (Jamaica)*

Brand/style	Size/ring	Flavor	Grade
Cetros	6 x 45	Medium	B+
Churchill	8 x 49	Medium	B+
Corona	5^{1}/$_{2}$ x 43	Medium	B+
Imperial	6^{1}/$_{2}$ x 45	Medium	B+
Lonsdale	6^{1}/$_{2}$ x 42	Medium	B+

* Sold through catalogs.

JOSE BENITO (Dominican Republic)

Brand/style	Size/ring	Flavor	Grade
Chico	4 x 36	Mild	A
Churchill	7 x 50	Medium	A
Corona	6^{3}/$_{4}$ x 43	Medium	A
Havanito	5 x 36	Mild	A
Magnum	8 x 64	Med–Full	A

Brand/style /country	Size/ ring	Flavor	Grade
Palma	6 x 34	Medium	A
Panatela	6³/₄ x 38	Medium	A
Petit	5¹/₂ x 38	Medium	A
Presidente	7³/₄ x 50	Med–Full	A
Rothschild	4¹/₂ x 50	Medium	A

JOSE MARTI (Dominican Republic)

Brand/style /country	Size/ ring	Flavor	Grade
Corona	5¹/₂ x 42	Medium	A-
Creme	6 x 35	Medium	A-
Maceo	6⁷/₈ x 45	Medium	A-
Marti	7¹/₂ x 50	Medium	A-
Palma	7 x 42	Medium	A-
Robusto	5¹/₂ x 50	Medium	A-

JOYA de NICARAGUA (Nicaragua)

Brand/style /country	Size/ ring	Flavor	Grade
Churchill	6⁷/₈ x 48	Medium	C
Consul	4¹/₂ x 52	Medium	C
Corona	5⁵/₈ x 48	Medium	C
Elegante	6¹/₂ x 38	Medium	C
National	5¹/₂ x 44	Medium	C
Petit Corona	5 x 42	Medium	C
Piccolino	4¹/₈ x 30	Medium	C
Presidente	8 x 54	Medium	C
Selection B	5¹/₂ x 42	Medium	C
Viajante	8¹/₂ x 52	Medium	C
No. 2	4¹/₂ x 41	Medium	C
5	6⁷/₈ x 35	Medium	C
10	6¹/₂ x 43	Medium	C

J.R. ULTIMATE (Honduras)*

Brand/style /country	Size/ ring	Flavor	Grade
Cetro	7 x 42	Medium	A
Corona	5.62 x 46	Medium	A
Double Corona	6³/₄ x 48	Medium	A
Estelo (individual)	8¹/₂ x 52	Med–Full	A
Palma Extra	6.88 x 38	Medium	A
Petit Cetro	5¹/₂ x 38	Medium	A
Petit Corona	4.62 x 43	Medium	A
President	8¹/₂ x 52	Med–Full	A
Rothschild	4¹/₂ x 50	Medium	A
Slims	6.88 x 36	Medium	A
Super Cetro	8 x 43	Medium	A

Brand/style /country	Size/ ring	Flavor	Grade
No. 1	7¹/₂ x 54	Medium	A
5	6.12 x 44	Medium	A
10	8¹/₄ x 47	Medium	A

*Sold through catalogs.

JUAN CLEMENTE (Dominican Republic)

Brand/style /country	Size/ ring	Flavor	Grade
Churchill	6⁷/₈ x 46	Mild	C
Club Selection			
No. 1	6 x 50	Mild	C
2	4³/₄ x 46	Mild	C
3	7 x 44	Mild	C
4	5¹/₄ x 42	Mild	C
Corona	5 x 42	Mild	C
Demi-Corona	4 x 40	Mild	C
Especiales	7¹/₂ x 38	Mild	C
Grand Corona	6 x 42	Mild	C
No. 530	5 x 30	Mild	C
Panatela	6¹/₂ x 34	Mild	C
Rothschild	4⁷/₈ x 50	Mild	C

JUAN LOPEZ (Cuba)
(FLOR DE JUAN LOPEZ)*

Brand/style /country	Size/ ring	Flavor	Grade
Corona	5⁵/₈ x 42	Mild	A
Patricia	4¹/₂ x 40	Mild	A
Petit Corona	5 x 42	Mild	A
Placera	5 x 34	Mild	A
Simarana	4³/₄ x 32	Mild	A

*No longer widely produced, found only in Spain.

KINGSTOWN (Mexico)

Brand/style /country	Size/ ring	Flavor	Grade
Corona Grande	6¹/₂ x 42	Med–Full	C+
Rothschild	4¹/₂ x 50	Med–Full	C+
Toro	6 x 50	Med–Full	C+

KNOCKANDO (Dominican Republic)

Brand/style /country	Size/ ring	Flavor	Grade
No. 1	6⁷/₈ x 45	Medium	A
2	6¹/₂ x 35	Medium	A
3	5⁵/₈ x 40	Mild	A
4	7¹/₂ x 48	Medium	A
St. James	5 x 42	Mild	A

Brand/style /country	Size/ ring	Flavor	Grade
LAS CABRILLAS (Honduras)			
Balboa	7½ x 54	Medium	B
Colombus	8½ x 52	Medium	B
Coronado	6.88 x 35	Medium	B
Cortez	4¾ x 50	Medium	B
De Soto	6.88 x 50	Medium	B
Magellan	6 x 42	Medium	B
Ponce de Leon	6.62 x 44	Medium	B
LA CORONA (Dominican Republic)			
American*	6½ x 34	Mild	A
Aristocrat*	6.12 x 36	Mild	A
Chica*	5½ x 42	Mild	A
Corona*	6.1 x 43	Mild	A
Demi Tasse*	4¼ x 39	Mild	A
Director*	6½ x 46	Mild	A
Whiff	3½ x 24	Mild	A

*Hard to find.

Brand/style /country	Size/ ring	Flavor	Grade
LA FINCA (Nicaragua)			
Bolivare	7½ x 50	Medium	C
Corona	5½ x 42	Medium	C
Flora	7 x 36	Medium	C
Hemingway	8½ x 52	Medium	C
Joya	6 x 50	Medium	C
Petit Corona	4½ x 42	Medium	C
Pico	6 x 36	Medium	C
Robusto	4½ x 50	Medium	C
Romeo	6½ x 42	Medium	C
LA FONTANA (Honduras)			
Dante	5½ x 38	Medium	B
Da Vinci	6.88 x 48	Medium	B
Galileo	5 x 50	Medium	B
Michelangelo	7½ x 52	Medium	B
Puccini	6½ x 44	Medium	B
Verdi	5½ x 44	Medium	B
LA FLOR de CANO (Cuba)*			
Corona	5 x 42	Mild	A-
Diademas (Churchill)	7 x 47	Mild	A-

Brand/style /country	Size/ ring	Flavor	Grade
Gran Corona	5⅝ x 46	Mild	A-
Short Churchill (robusto)	4⅞ x 50	Mild	A-

* Hard to find

Brand/style /country	Size/ ring	Flavor	Grade
LA FLOR DOMINICANA (Dominican Republic)			
Formerly Los Libertadores			
Alcalde	6½ x 44	Medium	A-
Diplomaticos	5 x 30	Medium	A-
Exilados	7½ x 38	Medium	A-
Insurrectos	5½ x 42	Medium	A-
Maceo	5 x 48	Medium	A-
Macheteros	4 x 40	Medium	A-
Mambises	6⅞ x 48	Medium	A-
LA GLORIA CUBANA (Cuba)*			
Cetros (Lonsdale)	6½ x 42	Full	A+
Medaille d'Or			
1 (panatela)	7⁵⁄₁₆ x 36	Full	A+
2 (Lonsdale)	6¹¹⁄₁₆ x 43	Full	A+
3	6⅞ x 28	Full	A+
4 (panatela)	6 x 32	Full	A+
Minutos	4½ x 40	Full	A+
Tainos (Churchill)	7 x 47	Full	A+
Tapados (Corona)	5⁵⁄₁₆ x 42	Full	A+
Sabrosas (Especial)	6⅛ x 42	Full	A+

*For another version see ratings—"Made in the USA"

Brand/style /country	Size/ ring	Flavor	Grade
LA INVICTA (Honduras)			
Churchill	6¾ x 47	Medium	A+
Corona	5½ x 42	Medium	A+
Magnum			
No. 2	5 x 50	Medium	A+
3	4½ x 50	Medium	A+
No. 10	5 x 50	Medium	A+
Petit Corona	5 x 42	Medium	A+

Brand/style /country	Size/ ring	Flavor	Grade
LA PRIMADORA (Honduras)			
Emperor	8¹/₂ x 50	Full	A
Excellentes	6¹/₂ x 42	Medium	A
Falcon	6¹/₂ x 34	Medium	A
Petit Cetro	5¹/₂ x 42	Medium	A
Solitaire	6 x 50	Full	A
Starbrite	4¹/₂ x 50	Medium	A
LA REGENTA (Canary Islands)			
Emperador	7¹/₂ x 52	Mild	A+
Findos	7 x 42	Mild	A+
Gran Corona	7¹/₄ x 46	Mild	A+
No. 1	6¹/₂ x 42	Mild	A+
2	6¹/₂ x 46	Mild	A+
3	5¹/₂ x 42	Mild	A+
4	5¹/₈ x 42	Mild	A+
Olimpicas	6¹/₈ x 36	Mild	A+
Premier	7 x 46	Mild	A+
Rothschild	4¹/₂ x 50	Mild	A+
LEON JIMENES (Dominican Republic)			
Robusto	5¹/₂ x 50	Full	A-
#1	7¹/₂ x 50	Full	A-
#2	7 x 47	Medium	A-
#3	6¹/₂ x 42	Medium	A-
#4	5¹⁹/₃₂ x 42	Medium	A-
#5	5 x 38	Medium	A-
LICENCIADOS (Dominican Republic)			
Excellentes	6³/₄ x 43	Medium	B
Panatela Linda	7 x 38	Medium	B
Presidente	8 x 50	Medium	B
Soberanos	8¹/₈ x 52	Medium	B
Supreme			
Maduro #200	5³/₄ x 43	Medium	B
#300	6³/₄ x 43	Medium	B
#400	6 x 50	Medium	B
#500	8 x 50	Medium	B
Toro	6 x 50	Medium	A
Wavell	5 x 50	Medium	B
#4	5³/₄ x 43	Medium	B
MACANUDO (Dominican Republic)			
Amatista	6¹/₂ x 42	Mild	A+
Ascot	4¹/₂ x 32	Mild	A+

Brand/style /country	Size/ ring	Flavor	Grade
Caviar	4 x 36	Mild	A+
Claridge	5¹/₂ x 38	Mild	A+
Claybourne	6 x 31	Mild	A+
Duke of Devon	5¹/₂ x 42	Mild	A+
Hampton			
Court	5³/₄ x 42	Mild	A+
Hyde Park	6 x 50	Mild	A+
Lonsdale	6³/₄ x 38	Mild	A+
Lord Claridge	5¹/₂ x 38	Mild	A+
Petit Corona	5 x 38	Mild	A+
Portofino	7 x 34	Mild	A+
Prince of			
Wales	8 x 50	Mild	A+
Prince Philip	7¹/₂ x 49	Mild	A+
Quill	5 x 28	Mild	A+
Rothschild	6¹/₂ x 42	Mild	A+
Somerset	7³/₄ x 31	Mild	A+
Sovereign	7 x 45	Mild	A+
Trumps	6¹/₂ x 48	Mild	A+
Vintage Cabinet			
No. 1	7¹/₂ x 49	Mild	A+
2	6.6 x 43	Mild	A+
3	5.6 x 43	Mild	A+
4	5 x 45	Mild	A+
5	5¹/₂ x 49	Mild	A+
7	8¹/₂ x 38	Mild	A+
MARIA MANCINI (Honduras)*			
Clemenceau	7 x 49	Medium	B
Corona Classic	5¹/₂ x 43	Medium	B
Corona Larga	6¹/₄ x 43	Medium	B
De Gaulle	6³/₄ x 43	Medium	B
Palma Delgado	7 x 39	Medium	B
Sold through catalogs.			
MATACAN (Mexico)			
No. 1	7¹/₂ x 50	Medium	B
2	6 x 50	Medium	B
3	6.62 x 46	Medium	B
4	6.62 x 42	Medium	B
5	6 x 42	Medium	B
6	6.62 x 35	Medium	B
7	4³/₄ x 50	Medium	B
8	8 x 52	Medium	B

Brand/style /country	Size/ring	Flavor	Grade
9	5 x 32	Medium	B
10	6.88 x 54	Medium	B

MOCAMBO (Mexico)*

Brand/style /country	Size/ring	Flavor	Grade
Churchill	7 x 50	Medium	A
Double Corona	6 x 51	Medium	A
Empires	6½ x 39	Medium	A
Premier	6⅝ x 43	Medium	A
Royal Corona	6 x 42	Mild	A
Santa Clara			
No. I	7 x 51	Medium	A
No. II	6½ x 48	Medium	A
No. III	6⅝ x 43	Medium	A
No. IV	5 x 44	Medium	A
No. V	6 x 44	Medium	A
No. VI	6 x 51	Medium	A
No. VII	5½ x 25	Medium	A
No. VIII	6½ x 30	Medium	A
Quino	4¼ x 30	Medium	

Sold through catalogs.

MOCHA SUPREME (Honduras)*

Brand/style /country	Size/ring	Flavor	Grade
Allegro	6½ x 36	Medium	A
Baron de Rothschild	4½ x 52	Medium	A
Lords	6½ x 42	Medium	A
Patron	7½ x 50	Full	A
Petites	4½ x 42	Medium	A
Rembrandt	8½ x 52	Full	A
Renaissance	6 x 50	Full	A
Sovereign	5½ x 42	Medium	A

Sold through catalogs.

MONTECRISTO (Cuba)

Brand/style /country	Size/ring	Flavor	Grade
Montecristo B	5⁵⁄₁₆ x 42	Medium	A+
Montecristo No. 1 (Lonsdale)	6½ x 42	Medium	A+
No. 2 (torpedo)	6⅛ x 52	Full	A+
No. 3 (Corona)	5½ x 42	Medium	A+
No. 4 (Petit corona)	5 x 42	Medium	A+
No. 5	4 x 40	Medium	A+
Montecristo Especial	7½ x 38	Full	A+
Montecristo Especial No. 2	6 x 38	Medium	A+

MONTECRISTO (Dominican Republic)

Brand/style /country	Size/ring	Flavor	Grade
Churchill	7 x 48	Medium	A
No. 1 Lonsdale	6½ x 42	Medium	A
No. 2 Torpedo	6 x 50	Medium	A
No. 3 Corona	5½ x 44	Medium	A
Robustos	4¾ x 50	Medium	A

MONTECRUZ (Dominican Republic)

Brand/style /country	Size/ring	Flavor	Grade
Cedar-aged	5 x 42	Medium	A+
Chicos	4 x 28	Medium	A+
Colossus	6½ x 50	Medium	A+
Individuales	8 x 46	Full	A+
Juniors	4⅞ x 33	Medium	A+
Montecruz A	6⅝ x 43	Medium	A+
Montecruz C	5⅝ x 43	Medium	A+
Montecruz D	7 x 36	Medium	A+
Montecruz F	7¼ x 47	Medium	A+
No. 200	7¼ x 46	Medium	A+
No. 205	7 x 42	Medium	A+
No. 210	6½ x 42	Medium	A+
No. 240	4¾ x 44	Medium	A+
No. 250	6 x 38	Medium	A+
No. 255	7 x 36	Medium	A+
No. 265	5½ x 38	Medium	A+
No. 280	7 x 28	Medium	A+
No. 282	5 x 28	Medium	A+
Robusto	4½ x 49	Medium	A+
Tubelares	6⅛ x 36	Medium	A+
Tubos	6 x 42	Medium	A+

MONTESINO (Dominican Republic)

Brand/style /country	Size/ring	Flavor	Grade
Diplomatico	5½ x 42	Mild	A
Fumas	6¾ x 44	Mild	A
Gran Corona	6¾ x 48	Mild	A
Napoleon Grande	7½ x 46	Medium	A

Brand/style /country	Size/ ring	Flavor	Grade
#1	$6^7/_8$ x 43	Mild	A
#2	$6^1/_4$ x 44	Mild	A
#3	$6^3/_4$ x 36	Mild	A
MONTEZUMA (Dominican Republic)			
Churchill	$6^7/_8$ x 50	Medium	A
Imperial	$8^1/_2$ x 50	Medium	A
Presidente	$7^1/_2$ x 50	Medium	A
NESTOR 747 (Honduras)			
Robusto	$4^3/_4$ x 54	Full	B+
Robusto Larga	6 x 54	Full	B+
747	$7^5/_8$ x 47	Full	B+
ONYX (Dominican Republic)			
#642	6 x 42	Medium	B
#646	$6^5/_8$ x 46	Medium	B
#650	6 x 50	Med–Full	B
#750	$7^1/_2$ x 50	Med–Full	B
#852	8 x 52	Med–Full	B
PADRON (Honduras)			
Ambassador	$6^7/_8$ x 42	Medium	B
Anniversary Series			
Corona	6 x 42	Medium	B
Diplomatico	7 x 50	Medium	B
Exclusivo	$5^1/_2$ x 50	Medium	B
Monarca	$6^1/_2$ x 46	Medium	B
Superior	$6^1/_2$ x 42	Medium	B
Churchill	$6^7/_8$ x 46	Medium	B
Delicias	$4^7/_8$ x 46	Medium	B
Executive	$7^1/_2$ x 50	Medium	B
Londres	$5^1/_2$ x 42	Medium	B
#2000	5 x 50	Medium	B
PARTAGAS (Cuba)			
Charlotte	$5^1/_2$ x 35	Full	A+
Churchill De Luxe	7 x 47	Full	A+
Corona	$5^1/_2$ x 42	Full	A+
Corona Grande	6 x 42	Full	A+
Culebras (twisted)	$5^{11}/_{16}$ x 39	Full	A+

Brand/style /country	Size/ ring	Flavor	Grade
Lonsdale	$6^1/_2$ x 42	Full	A+
Lusitanias	$7^5/_8$ x 49	Full	A+
Palmas Grandes	7 x 33	Full	A+
Partagas de Partagas No. 1	$6^{11}/_{16}$ x 43	Full	A+
Petit Corona	5 x 42	Full	A+
Selecion Privada No. 1	$6^{11}/_{16}$ x 43	Full	A+
Series D No. 4	$4^7/_8$ x 50	Full	A+
Shorts	$4^5/_{16}$ x 42	Full	A+
Tres Petit Corona	$4^1/_2$ x 40	Full	A+
8-9-8	$6^{11}/_{16}$ x 43	Full	A+
PARTAGAS (Dominican Republic)			
Almirante	$6^1/_4$ x 47	Full	A+
Humitube	$6^3/_4$ x 44	Full	A+
Maduro	$6^1/_4$ x 47	Full	A+
Naturale	$5^1/_2$ x 50	Full	A+
Puritos	$4^1/_4$ x 32	Full	A+
Robusto	$4^1/_2$ x 49	Full	A+
Sabroso	$5^3/_4$ x 43	Full	A+
#1	$6^3/_4$ x 43	Full	A+
#2	$5^3/_4$ x 43	Full	A+
#3	$5^1/_4$ x 43	Full	A+
#4	5 x 38	Full	A+
#5	$5^1/_8$ x 50	Full	A+
#6	6 x 47	Full	A+
#10	$7^1/_2$ x 49	Full	A+
8-9-8	$6^7/_8$ x 44	Full	A+
Limited Reserve			
Regale	$6^1/_4$ x 47	Full	A+
Royale	$6^3/_4$ x 43	Full	A+
PAUL GARMIRIAN GOURMET (Dominican Republic)			
Belicoso	$6^1/_2$ x 52	Full	A
Belicoso Fino	$5^3/_4$ x 52	Medium	A
Celebration	9 x 50	Full	A
Churchill	7 x 48	Full	A
Connoisseur	6 x 50	Medium	A

Brand/style /country	Size/ ring	Flavor	Grade
Corona	5¾ x 42	Medium	A
Double Corona	7⅝ x 50	Full	A
Epicure	5¾ x 50	Medium	A
Lonsdale	5 x 50	Medium	A
Petit Bouquet	4¾ x 38	Medium	A
Robusto	5 x 50	Medium	A
No. 1	6½ x 38	Medium	A
2	4¾ x 48	Medium	A
5	4 x 40	Medium	A

PLEIADES (Dominican Republic)

Brand/style /country	Size/ ring	Flavor	Grade
Aldebran	8½ x 50	Mild	A
Antares	5½ x 40	Mild	A
Mars	5 x 28	Mild	A
Neptune	7½ x 42	Mild	A
Orion	5¾ x 42	Mild	A
Perseus	5 x 34	Mild	A
Pluton	5 x 50	Mild	A
Saturne	8 x 46	Mild	A
Sirius	6⅞ x 46	Mild	A
Uranus	6⅞ x 34	Mild	A

POR LARRANAGA (Dominican Republic)

Brand/style /country	Size/ ring	Flavor	Grade
Corona	5½ x 42	Med–Full	A+
Lonsdale	6½ x 42	Med–Full	A+
Petit Corona	5 x 42	Med–Full	A+
Small Corona	4½ x 40	Med–Full	A+

PRIMO del REY (Dominican Republic)

Brand/style /country	Size/ ring	Flavor	Grade
Almirante	6 x 50	Mild–Med	A+
Aquila	8 x 52	Mild–Med	A+
Aristocrats	6¾ x 48	Mild–Med	A+
Barons	8½ x 52	Mild–Med	A+
Cazadore	6.15 x 44	Mild–Med	A+
Chavon	6½ x 41	Mild–Med	A+
Churchill	6¼ x 48	Mild–Med	A+
Corto Tins	4 x 28	Mild–Med	A+
Nobles	6¼ x 44	Mild–Med	A+
Panatela	5.37 x 34	Mild–Med	A+
Panatela Extra	6 x 34	Mild–Med	A+
President	6¾ x 44	Mild–Med	A+
Reale	6.12 x 36	Mild–Med	A+

Brand/style /country	Size/ ring	Flavor	Grade
Regals	7 x 50	Mild–Med	A+
Soberano	7½ x 50	Mild–Med	A+
No. 1	6¾ x 42	Mild–Med	A+
2	6¼ x 42	Mild–Med	A+
3	6¾ x 36	Mild–Med	A+
4	5½ x 42	Mild–Med	A+
100	4½ x 50	Mild–Med	A+

PUNCH (Cuba)

Brand/style /country	Size/ ring	Flavor	Grade
Churchill	7 x 47	Mild–Med	A+
Corona	5⅝ x 42	Mild–Med	A+
Diademas Extra	9¼ x 47	Medium	A+
Double Corona	7⅝ x 49	Medium	A+
Gran Corona	$5^{11/16}$ x 40	Mild–Med	A+
Margarita	4¼ x 26	Mild–Med	A+
Panatela	7 x 49	Mild–Med	A+
Petit Corona	5 x 42	Mild–Med	A+
Petit Punch	4 x 40	Mild	A+
Punch Punch	5½ x 46	Mild–Med	A+
Royal Selection No. 11	5½ x 46	Mild–Med	A+
Royal Selection No. 12	5 x 42	Mild–Med	A+
Selection De Luxe No. 2	5 x 42	Mild–Med	A+
Super Selection No. 1	6 x 42	Mild–Med	A+
No. 2	5½ x 40	Mild–Med	A+

PUNCH (Honduras)

Brand/style /country	Size/ ring	Flavor	Grade
After Dinner	7½ x 45	Full	A
Amatista	6.12 x 44	Full	A
Bristol	6¼ x 44	Full	A
Britania	6¼ x 50	Full	A
Cafe Royale	5¼ x 44	Full	A
Casa Grande	7¼ x 46	Full	A
Chateau Corona	6½ x 44	Full	A
Lafitte	7¼ x 52	Full	A
Margaux	5½ x 46	Full	A

Brand/style /country	Size/ ring	Flavor	Grade
Double Corona	6³/₄ x 48	Full	A
Diademas	7¹/₂ x 36	Full	A
Elite	5¹/₂ x 44	Full	A
Largo Elegant	7.12 x 32	Full	A
London Club	5 x 40	Full	A
Monarcas	6³/₄ x 48	Full	A
No. 75	5¹/₂ x 44	Full	A
Pita	6¹/₂ x 50	Full	A
Presidente	8¹/₂ x 52	Full	A
Prince Consort	8¹/₂ x 52	Full	A
Punch	6.12 x 44	Full	A
Rothschild	4¹/₂ x 48	Full	A
Royal Coronations	5.62 x 44	Full	A
Slim Panatela	4 x 28	Full	A
Super Rothschild	5 x 48	Full	A
Superiore	5.62 x 46	Full	A

QUORUM (Dominican Republic)*

Chairman	7¹/₂ x 50	Mild–Med	A
Corona	5.62 x 42	Mild–Med	A-
No. 1	6 x 42	Mild–Med	A
President	7¹/₄ x 46	Mild–Med	A
Rothschild	4¹/₂ x 50	Mild–Med	A
Trump	4¹/₄ x 42	Mild–Med	A
Whillo	7 x 36	Mild–Med	A-

* Sold through catalog.

RAMON ALLONES (Cuba)

Corona	5⁵/₈ x 42	Full	A+
Coronas Gigantes	7¹/₂ x 49	Full	A+
Panatela	5 x 35	Full	A+
Petit Corona	5 x 42	Full	A+
Ramonitas	4¹³/₁₆ x 26	Full	A+
Small Club Coronas	4⁵/₁₆ x 42	Full	A+
Specially Selected (Robusto)	4¹¹/₁₆ x 50	Full	A+
8-9-8 (Churchill)	6¹¹/₁₆ x 43	Full	A+

Brand/style /country	Size/ ring	Flavor	Grade
RAMON ALLONES (Dominican Republic)			
Crystal	6¹/₄ x 43	Medium	A
Redondo	7 x 49	Medium	A
Size A	7 x 45	Medium	A
B	6¹/₂ x 42	Medium	A
D	5 x 42	Medium	A
Trump	6³/₄ x 43	Medium	A

RIATA (Honduras)

No. 100	7 x 30	Medium	C
No. 200	6⁷/₈ x 35	Medium	C
No. 300	6 x 42	Medium	C
No. 400	5¹/₂ x 44	Medium	C
No. 500	6⁵/₈ x 44	Medium	C
No. 600	6⁷/₈ x 44	Medium	C
No. 700	4³/₄ x 50	Medium	C
No. 800	6¹/₄ x 50	Medium	C
No. 900	7¹/₂ x 50	Medium	C
No. 1000	8¹/₂ x 52	Medium	C

ROMEO y JULIETA (Cuba)

Belicosos	5¹/₂ x 52	Mild	A+
Cedros de Luxe No. 1	6¹/₂ x 42	Mild	A+
No. 2	5¹/₂ x 42	Mild	A+
No. 3	5 x 42	Mild	A+
Churchill	7 x 47	Medium	A+
Clemenceau	7 x 47	Medium	A+
Corona	5¹/₂ x 42	Mild	A+
Corona Grande	6 x 42	Mild	A+
Exhibicion No. 3	5¹/₂ x 43	Mild	A+
No. 4 (Robusto)	5 x 48	Mild	A+
Petit Julietas	4 x 30	Mild	A+
Prince of Wales	7 x 47	Medium	A+
Shakespeare	6⁷/₈ x 28	Mild	A+
Tres Petit Corona	4¹/₂ x 40	Mild	A+

ROMEO y JULIETA (Honduras)

Celestiales	8 x 36	Full	A+
Gigante	7 x 48	Full	A+

Brand/style /country	Size/ ring	Flavor	Grade	Brand/style /country	Size/ ring	Flavor	Grade
Especiales	6¼ x 43	Medium	A+	Navarro	6¾ x 34	Mild	A+
Prado	5½ x 42	Medium	A+	Park Lane	6 x 47	Mild	A+
Princessa	5¼ x 39	Medium	A+	Petit Corona	5 x 40	Mild	A+
Sublime	4½ x 50	Medium	A+	Pirate	4½ x 30	Mild	A+
				Robusto	4½ x 49	Mild	A+
				Royal Corona	6 x 40	Mild	A+
				Tube #1	6 x 45	Mild	A+
				Tube #2	6⅜ x 34	Mild	A+

ROMEO y JULIETA (Dominican Republic)

Brand/style	Size/ring	Flavor	Grade
Breva	5.62 x 38	Mild	A+
Cetro	6½ x 44	Mild	A+
Chiquita	4¼ x 32	Mild	A+
Churchill	7 x 50	Medium	A+
Corona	5½ x 44	Mild	A+
Delgado	7 x 32	Mild	A+
Monarca	8 x 52	Medium	A+
Panatela	5¼ x 35	Mild	A+
President	7 x 43	Medium	A+
Rothschild	5 x 50	Medium	A+
Vintage #1	6 x 43	Mild	A+
#2	6 x 46	Mild	A+
#3	4½ x 50	Mild	A+
#4	7 x 48	Medium	A+
#5	7½ x 50	Medium	A+

ROYAL DOMINICANA (Dominican Republic)

Brand/style	Size/ring	Flavor	Grade
Churchill	7¼ x 50	Medium	A
Corona	6 x 46	Medium	A
Minis	4¼ x 40	Mild	A
Nacional	5½ x 43	Mild	A
No. 1	6¼ x 43	Mild	A
Super Fino	6 x 35	Mild	A

ROYAL JAMAICA (Dominican Republic)

Brand/style	Size/ring	Flavor	Grade
Buccaneer	5½ x 30	Mild	A+
Churchill	8 x 51	Mild	A+
Corona	5½ x 40	Mild	A+
Corona Grande	6½ x 42	Mild	A+
Director #1	6 x 45	Mild	A+
Double Corona	7 x 45	Mild	A+
Doubloon	7 x 30	Mild	A+
Gaucho	5¼ x 33	Mild	A+
Giant Corona	7½ x 49	Mild	A+
Goliath	9 x 64	Mild	A+

SAINT LUIS REY (Cuba)

(Not to be confused with San Luis Rey, Cuban-made for the German market)

Brand/style	Size/ring	Flavor	Grade
Churchill	7 x 47	Full	A+
Corona	5⅝ x 42	Full	A+
Lonsdale	6½ x 42	Full	A+
Petit Corona	5 x 42	Full	A+
Regios (Robusto)	5 x 48	Full	A+

SANCHO PANZA (Cuba)

Brand/style	Size/ring	Flavor	Grade
Bachilleres	4⅝ x 40	Mild	A+
Belicosos	5½ x 52	Mild	A+
Corona	5⅝ x 42	Mild	A+
Corona Gigante	7 x 47	Mild	A+
Molino (Lonsdale)	6½ x 42	Mild	A+
Non Plus Petit Corona	5¹⁄₁₆ x 42	Mild	A+
Panatela Largo	6½ x 28	Mild	A+

SAN CRISTOBAL (Dominican Republic)

Brand/style	Size/ring	Flavor	Grade
#200	5½ x 43	Medium	A
#300	6¾ x 43	Medium	A
#400	6¾ x 48	Medium	A
#500	7½ x 50	Full	A

SANTA CLARA (Mexico)

Brand/style	Size/ring	Flavor	Grade
I	7 x 51	Medium	A-
II	6½ x 48	Medium	A-
III	6.62 x 43	Medium	A-
IV	5 x 44	Medium	A-
V	6 x 44	Medium	A-

Brand/style /country	Size/ ring	Flavor	Grade
VI	6 x 51	Medium	A-
VII	$5^1/_2$ x 25	Medium	A-
VIII	$6^1/_2$ x 30	Medium	A-
Quino	$4^1/_4$ x 30	Medium	A-
SANTA CRUZ (Jamaica)			
Bristol	$6^3/_4$ x 45	Medium	B+
Churchill	6 x 50	Medium	B+
Corona	$5^1/_2$ x 42	Medium	B+
Corona Grande	$6^1/_2$ x 42	Medium	B+
Majestic	$6^3/_4$ x 38	Medium	B+
Palmetta	6 x 31	Medium	B+
SANTA DAMIANA (Dominican Republic)			
Selecion 100	$6^3/_4$ x 48	Mild	A+
200 (Corona)	$5^1/_2$ x 42	Mild	A+
300	$5^1/_2$ x 46	Mild	A+
400 (Petit Corona)	5 x 42	Mild	A+
500 (Robusto)	5 x 50	Mild	A+
600 (Très Petit Corona)	$4^1/_2$ x 36	Mild	A+
700	$6^1/_2$ x 42	Mild	A+
800	7 x 50	Mild	A+
SAVINELLI EXTRA LIMITED RESERVE (Dominican Republic)			
Introduced in 1994, these cigars were the first to be marketed by a company known for pipes. They are made for the New Jersey firm by A. Fuente in the Dominican Republic.			
#1—Churchill	$7^1/_4$ x 48	Full	A
#2—Corona Extra	$6^5/_8$ x 46	Full	A
#3—Lonsdale	$6^1/_4$ x 43	Full	A
#4—Double Corona	6 x 50	Full	A
#5—Extraor dinaire	$5^1/_4$ x 44	Full	A
#6—Robusto	5 x 49	Full	A

Brand/style /country	Size/ ring	Flavor	Grade
SCHIMMELPENNICK (Holland)			
Duet			
Brasil	$5^1/_2$ x 27	Medium	A
Drum	5.62 x 27	Medium	A
Regular	5.62 x 27	Medium	A
Florina	3.88 x 36	Mild	A
Half Corona	$3^3/_4$ x 36	Medium	A
Media	3.12 x 26	Mild	A
Mini Cigars	$2^3/_4$ x 26	Mild	A
Mono	3.37 x 27	Mild	A
Nostra	2.88 x 27	Mild	A
Vada	3.88 x 30	Mild	A
SHAKESPEARE (Dominican Republic)			
Ambassador	$7^1/_2$ x 49	Medium	A
Breva	$5^3/_4$ x 43	Mild	A
Diplomat	$6^3/_4$ x 43	Medium	A
Panatela	6 x 34	Mild	A
SOSA (Dominican Republic)			
Brevas	$5^1/_2$ x 43	Medium	B
Churchill	$6^{15}/_{16}$ x 48	Medium	B
Governor	6 x 50	Medium	B
Lonsdale	$6^1/_2$ x 43	Medium	B
Magnum	$7^1/_2$ x 52	Full	B
Piramide #2	7 x 64	Medium	B
Santa Fe	6 x 35	Medium	B
Wavell	$4^3/_4$ x 50	Medium	B
SPECIAL CORONAS (Dominican Republic)*			
No. 2	$6^1/_2$ x 45	Mild	A+
No. 4	$5^1/_2$ x 45	Mild	A+
No. 54	6 x 54	Medium	A+
No. 754	7 x 54	Medium	A+
Pyramides	7 x 54	Medium	A+
**Sold through catalogs.*			
SPECIAL JAMAICANS (Dominican Republic)*			
Bonita	6 x 50	Mild	A
Churchill	7 x 52	Mild	A

Brand/style /country	Size/ ring	Flavor	Grade
Fancytale	6$\frac{1}{2}$ x 43	Mild	A
Mayfair	7 x 60	Mild	A
Nobles	7 x 50	Mild	A
Pica	5 x 32	Mild	A
Pyramid	7 x 52	Mild	A
Rey del Rey	9 x 60	Mild	A
Size A	6$\frac{1}{2}$ x 44	Mild	A
B	6 x 44	Mild	A
C	5$\frac{1}{2}$ x 44	Mild	A
D	6 x 50	Mild	A

Sold through catalogs.

SUERDIECK (Brazil)

Brand/style	Size/ring	Flavor	Grade
Brasilia	5$\frac{3}{4}$ x 30	Mild	C
Caballero	6 x 30	Mild	C
Fiesta	6 x 30	Mild	C
Mandarim Pai	5 x 38	Mild	C
NIP	6 x 30	Mild	C
Valencia	6 x 30	Mild	C

TE-AMO (Mexico)

Brand/style	Size/ring	Flavor	Grade
C.E.O	8$\frac{1}{2}$ x 52	Full	C
Caballero	7 x 35	Full	C
Churchill	7$\frac{1}{2}$ x 50	Full	C
Elegante	5$\frac{1}{2}$ x 30	Full	C
Epicure	5 x 27	Full	C
Impulse	5 x 32	Full	C
Intermezzo	4 x 28	Full	C
Maximo	7 x 54	Full	C
Meditation	6 x 42	Full	C
No. 4	5 x 42	Full	C
Picadore	7 x 27	Full	C
Presidente	7 x 50	Full	C
Relaxation	6$\frac{5}{8}$ x 44	Full	C
Robusto	5$\frac{1}{2}$ x 54	Full	C
Satisfaction	6 x 46	Full	C
Torero	6$\frac{1}{2}$ x 35	Full	C
Torito	4$\frac{1}{2}$ x 50	Full	C
Toro	6 x 50	Full	C

TEMPLE HALL (Jamaica)

Brand/style	Size/ring	Flavor	Grade
#450 (Robusto)	4$\frac{1}{2}$ x 49	Mild	A+
#500	5 x 31	Mild	A+
#550	5$\frac{1}{2}$ x 50	Medium	A+

Brand/style /country	Size/ ring	Flavor	Grade
#625 (Corona Grande)	6$\frac{1}{4}$ x 42	Medium	A+
#675	6$\frac{3}{4}$ x 45	Medium	A+
#685 (Panatela)	6$\frac{7}{8}$ x 34	Mild	A+
#700 (Churchill)	7 x 49	Medium	A+
4030	6$\frac{1}{4}$ x 42	Medium	A+
4031	6$\frac{3}{4}$ x 42	Medium	A+
4032	6 x 45	Medium	A+
4033	7 x 45	Medium	A+

TENA y VEGA (Costa Rica)

Brand/style	Size/ring	Flavor	Grade
Cetros	6$\frac{3}{8}$ x 43	Medium	A-
Churchill	7 x 50	Full	A-
Double Corona	6 x 50	Full	A
No. 1	7 x 44	Full	A-

TORCEDOR (Nicaragua)

Brand/style	Size/ring	Flavor	Grade
#1	7 x 44	Full	B
Churchill	7 x 50	Full	B
Toro	6 x 50	Full	B
Rothchild	5 x 50	Full	B
Viajante	8 x 52	Full	B

TRESADO (Dominican Republic)

Brand/style	Size/ring	Flavor	Grade
No. 100	8 x 52	Medium	A
200	7 x 48	Medium	A
300	6 x 46	Medium	A
400	6.62 x 44	Medium	A
500	5$\frac{1}{2}$ x 42	Medium	A

TRINIDAD (Cuba)

Not for sale: one size, made exclusively for Fidel Castro! It's not known if the U.S. Central Intelligence Agency had one of these in mind as part of the alleged plan to get rid of Castro by having someone slip him either a poisoned or an exploding cigar. Fidel's doctors have since forbidden him to smoke anything.

VERACRUZ (Mexico)

Brand/style	Size/ring	Flavor	Grade
Magnum	7$\frac{7}{8}$ x 48	Medium	B+

Brand/style /country	Size/ ring	Flavor	Grade
Mina de Veracruz	6¼ x 42	Medium	B+
VUELTABAJO (Dominican Republic)			
Churchill	7 x 48	Medium	B
Corona	5¾ x 42	Medium	B
Gigante	8½ x 50	Full	B
Lonsdale	7 x 43	Medium	B
Robusto	4¾ x 52	Medium	B
Toro	6 x 50	Medium	B
WHITEHALL (Jamaica)			
Corona Deluxe	5¾ x 42	Medium	B
Finos Deluxe	6 x 32	Medium	B
Grand Duke	6⅞ x 38	Medium	B
Lonsdale Deluxe	6½ x 42	Medium	B

Brand/style /country	Size/ ring	Flavor	Grade
ZINO (Honduras)			
Connoisseur 100	7¾ x 50	Medium	A
Connoisseur 200	7½ x 46	Medium	A
Connoisseur 300	5¾ x 46	Mild	A
Diamond	5½ x 40	Mild	A
Elegance	6¾ x 34	Medium	A
Junior	6½ x 30	Medium	A
Mouton Cadet No. 1	6½ x 44	Mild	A
Mouton Cadet No. 2	6 x 35	Mild	A
Mouton Cadet No. 3	5¾ x 36	Mild	A
Princesse	4½ x 20	Mild	A
Tradition	6¼ x 44	Medium	A
Veritas	7 x 50	Medium	A

Made in the USA

When Depression-era humorist Will Rogers quipped that the United States was the only country in history to go to the poorhouse in an automobile, he could have added that the men of America could do so while puffing on what Vice President Marshall had wished for—a good five-cent cigar. Just as Henry Ford had put a car within reach of the average citizen, inventors such as Oscar Hammerstein and cigar manufacturers such as the Paley family had created, by the 1930s, a line of machine-made cigars that made the United States the biggest market for cigars in the world. Though very few of those inexpensive smokes could compete in quality with the hand-rolled premiums of Cuba and the other countries of the Caribbean, neither could a Ford or a Chevrolet match the luxuries of a Rolls or a Deusenberg. But what American cars and the domestic cigar represented is exactly what the United States stood for—democratic government and democracy in the marketplace, and that includes cigars.

Although it is always risky to generalize, we feel secure in stating that the inexpensive domestic cigars that dominate the American market are consistent in construction and uniformly mild/sweet in flavor. Considered in those terms, and if price is a key factor in what you smoke, they can be a reliable buy.

The following are among leading domestics of today, arranged by brand, style, and size (including a few handmades):

Brand/style	Size/ring
ANTELO (Handmade, Miami)	
Churchill	$6^7/_8$ x 46
Panatela	$6^7/_8$ x 46
Wavell	$5^1/_8$ x 46
ANTONIO y CLEOPATRA (Puerto Rico	
Grenadier	$6^1/_4$ x 33
Miniature	$4^1/_2$ x 33
Panatela	$5^1/_2$ x 35
President	$5^1/_2$ x 44
CARIBBEAN ROUND	
Casino	$6^1/_2$ x 43
Petit	4.88 x 36
Royale	$6^1/_2$ x 36
Round	$7^1/_4$ x 45
CHAVELO (Handmade, Miami)	
Churchill	$6^7/_8$ x 50
Panatela	$6^5/_8$ x 36
Presidente	$7^3/_8$ x 50
DUTCH MASTERS	
This cigar regularly outsells all handmade cigars in the United States. A typical year's volume exceeds 100 million.	
Belvedere	5.62 x 42
Cadet Tip	5 x 28

Brand/style	Size/ring
Corona	$5^3/_4$ x 44
Elite	6 x 36
Palma	5.62 x 42
Panatela	$5^1/_2$ x 36
Perfecto	$4^3/_4$ x 42
President	5.62 x 42
DUTCH TREATS	
Machine made ($3^7/_8$ x 20) and available in regular, menthol, pipe aroma, sweet, and Ultra Lite flavors.	
EDEN	
Corona DeLuxe	6 x 43
Directors	$7^3/_4$ x 45
Exquisito	$6^1/_2$ x 36
Palma Royale	6 x 42
No. 1	$7^1/_4$ x 44
EL PRODUCTO	
Made by the same company as Dutch Masters.	
Backwoods	$4^1/_2$ x 32
Blunt	5.12 x 42
Boquet	$4^3/_4$ x 42
Corona	$5^3/_4$ x 42
Escepcional	$5^1/_2$ x 48
Fino	4.88 x 44
Li'l Corona	4.62 x 28

LA HOYA SELECTA

Cetra de Oro	5³/₄ x 43
Choix Supreme	6 x 50
Cosiac	7 x 48
Palais Royale	4³/₄ x 50

KING EDWARD

Cigarillo Deluxe	4¹/₄ x 281/2
Imperial	5 x 41
Invincible Deluxe	5¹/₂ x 42
Panatela Deluxe	5¹/₄ x 36
Wood Tip Cigarillo	5¹/₂ x 29

LA EMINENCIA (Handmade, Tampa)

After Dinner (Churchill)	8 x 48
Baron	5¹/₄ x 48
Premier	7 x 44
Supreme	8¹/₂ x 52

LA GLORIA CUBANA

Charlemagne	7¹/₄ x 54
Churchill	7 x 50
Soberano	8 x 52
Torpedo	6¹/₂ x 52
Wavell	5 x 50

LA ISLA (Handmade, Union City, New Jersey)

Corona	7 x 46
Especiale	7 x 46
Fumas	6³/₄ x 44
Palmas	7 x 36
Panatela	6¹/₄ x 35

LA PLATA (Handmade, Los Angeles, California)

Brazilian Churchill	7¹/₄ x 54
Dessert Special	5 x 36
Enterprise	7 x 52
Hamiltons	8 x 42
Pyramid	7 x 50
Rocket	8 x 50
Victor No. 1	7 x 46
Victor No. 2	5 x 50

LAS VEGAS CIGAR COMPANY (Handmade, Las Vegas, Nevada)

Churchill	7¹/₂ x 50
Corona	5³/₄ x 42
Excalibur	8³/₄ x 52
Imperial	7 x 48
Palma	7 x 38
Panatela	6¹/₄ x 36
Rothschild	4¹/₂ x 50

LORD BEACONSFIELD

Cubanola	5¹/₂ x 44
Director	7³/₄ x 45
Linda	6¹/₂ x 36
Lord	7 x 34
Round	7¹/₄ x 46
No. 1	6¹/₄ x 43
4	7¹/₄ x 45
10	7¹/₄ x 45

LORD CLINTON (Unrelated to the President of the U.S.)

Panatela	5¹/₄ x 34
Perfecto	5 x 42¹/₂

MURIEL

Perhaps best known for its television commercials featuring Edie Adams (widow of the cigar-smoking comedian Ernie Kovacs). Adams sold a lot of Muriels, and at the same time opened some American minds to the idea that it's okay for a woman to light up a cigar, although she never actually smoked one on the air. Made in Puerto Rico.

Airtip	4¹/₂ x 30
Cigarillo	4 x 30
Cigarillo Tip	4 x 30
Corona	5 x 40
Magnum	5¹/₂ x 44
Mini	4 x 30
Panatela	5 x 36

STATE
OF
THE
CIGAR

Brand/style	Size/ring

OPTIMO

Its makers proved that putting the name of its cigar on a sign in the front of a store is a good way to sell cigars.

Admiral	6 x 42
Corona	5^1/$_2$ x 42
Palma	6 x 42
Panatela	5 x 36
Sport	4^1/$_2$ x 42

PHILLIES

Blunt*	5 x 40
Cheroot	5 x 32
Corona	5^3/$_8$ x 41
Mexicali Slim	4^5/$_8$ x 32
Sport	5^3/$_4$ x 43

The popular Blunts had the misfortune to be adopted by college students in the 1990s as a method of smoking marijuana by hollowing out the foot of the cigar and replacing the tobacco with the dope.

ROBERT BURNS

In 1993 sales of this perennial favorite's corona-sized "Black Watch," in packages of three cedar-lined aluminum tubes, reached 52 million.

ROI-TAN (Puerto Rico)

Banker	5 x 40^1/$_2$
Blunt	5^5/$_8$ x 40^1/$_2$
Falcon	6^1/$_4$ x 33^1/$_2$
Panatela	5^1/$_2$ x 36
Perfecto Extra	5 x 40^1/$_2$
Cigarillo Tip	5^1/$_8$ x 27

SWISHER SWEETS

Cigarillo	4 x 30
Coronella	4 x 30
King	5 x 40
Outlaw	4 x 30
Perfecto	5 x 40
Slim	4^1/$_2$ x 30

Brand/style	Size/ring
Tip Cigarillo	4^1/$_2$ x 30
Wood Tip	5 x 30

TAMPA CUB

Gem	5 x 42^1/$_2$
Straight	5 x 42^1/$_2$

TAMPA NUGGET

Blunt	5 x 43
Junior	4^1/$_2$ x 31
Miniature	4^1/$_2$ x 31
Panatela	5^1/$_2$ x 36
Sublime	4^3/$_4$ x 43
Tipped	5 x 28

TAMPA SWEET

Cheroot	4^3/$_4$ x 31
Perfecto	4^3/$_4$ x 43
Tipped Cigarillo	5 x 28

TIPARILLO and TIJUANA

Another widely advertised brand, the Tiparillo is, of course, tipped with a plastic holder. Both brands offer smokers a choice of flavors.

Tijuana Small	4 x 26
in Aromatic, Cherry, or Regular	
Tiparillo	5 x 30
in Aromatic, Menthol, Regular, or Sweet	

TOPPER

Breva	5^1/$_2$ x 45
Ebony	5^1/$_2$ x 44
Grand Corona	6 x 44
Old Fashioned Perfecto	4^7/$_8$ x 44

TOPSTONE (Connecticut Broadleaf Series)

Boquet	5^1/$_2$ x 46
Directors	7^3/$_4$ x 47
Extra Oscuro	5^1/$_2$ x 46
Grande	5^3/$_4$ x 46
Oscuro	5^1/$_2$ x 46
Panatela	6 x 39
Supreme	6 x 42

Brand/style	Size/ring	Brand/style	Size/ring
VILLA de CUBA		Blunt	5 x 42
		Coronetta	5 x 30
Chica	5¹/₂ x 45	Demi Tip	4¹/₂ x 28
Monarch	7 x 46	Invincible	5¹/₄ x 42
Palma	6¹/₂ x 43	Miniature	4 x 28
VILLAZON DELUXE		Mini Sweet	4 x 28
		New Yorker	5¹/₂ x 42
Cetro	7¹/₈ x 44	Ranger	5¹/₂ x 34
Chairman	7³/₄ x 43	**WILLIAM PENN**	
Senator	6³/₄ x 44	Brave	5 x 40
WHITE OWL		Panatela	5¹/₄ x 34

Arguably the most recognized brand in the United States, even among nonsmokers, it was one of the first brands to suggest in its ads that not all women hated cigars and that some even found them to be sexy. One featured a sultry towel-wrapped beauty who apparently had just stepped from the shower. Shown with an unlit White Owl miniature between her lips and a pack of them tucked under the back of the towel, she stated, "If I were a man, I'd smoke White Owl Miniatures. If you are a man, take up with the small, trim, good-looking cigar that makes you look good."

White Owls are available as:

Brand/style	Size/ring
Perfecto	5¹/₄ x 40
Willowtip	4¹/₂ x 28
HOUSE of WINDSOR and MARK IV	
Crooks	5 x 40
Imperial	8 x 43
Maduro Suprema	6¹/₂ x 43
Magnate	6¹/₂ x 43
Palma	6¹/₂ x 43
Panatela	6¹/₂ x 34
Sportsmen	5 x 43

If there is one generality concerning American-made cigars, other than their moderate prices, it is that they are short in length. The vast majority sold are pocket-sized. This may reflect the stereotypical portrait of the average American as always on the go and, therefore, not having the leisure to savor a long cigar even if he wanted to. But in choosing the shorter smoke the trade-off is in the flavor. The challenge confronting all makers of small ring gauge cigars, including those who produce the top-of-the-line handmade premiums, is that a thinner girth makes it difficult to attain a blend that delivers complexity and strength of flavor. Compromises in taste and texture are also required in making cigars by machine. It is far more likely to find voids in a machined cigar than in a hand-rolled, resulting in unpleasant hot spots. Because most of these cigars are purchased in packages, it is impossible to test them for uniformity in the firmness of their filler. Nor can the buyer expect that the wrapper will be of the highest quality. But problems with short cigars are not limited to machine-made American brands. The editors of *CIGAR Aficionado* magazine rated premium short cigars (petite coronas of 5–5$\frac{1}{2}$ inches, 38 to 42 ring gauge) and found that of the seventy-four brands evaluated, all fell in the midrange of their scoring on a scale of 100 points. None reached the 90s. There was also a high rate of construction flaws. Like the low-priced domestics, premiums, in the view of the surveyors, gave "a modest amount of smoking pleasure . . . in a short period of time."

As in every other aspect of cigar smoking, size is a matter of personal preference, although the range of choice may be constrained by the realities of one's pocketbook. But even if economic status dictates the daily smoking of the varieties of domestic, machine-made brands at the low end of the spectrum, it does not have to be that big a leap into the world of premiums.

A fine handmade Dominican can be bought for the same price as a five-pack of ordinary domestics, so an occasional "splurge" can be worth it. Or by simply taking to heart the old adage "a penny saved is a penny earned," accumulated pocket change can result in a glorious smoke. And there is something to be said for informing loved ones that for your birthday, Christmas, or Hanukkah gift the cost of an excellent cigar is the same price as that same old necktie or bottle of aftershave lotion.

You might also propose that the costs of several gifts could be combined instead for the purchase of a *box* of premiums. Of course, if you undertake such an enterprise, be sure to make clear the brand and type preferred. You don't want the choice of cigar going as dreadfully amiss as some selections of ties and aftershave do.

As in the buying of a single cigar, there are guidelines for the purchase of cigars by the box. They are generally available in quantities of ten, twenty-five, fifty, and one hundred. Many of the brands are stacked in alternate rows known as 8-9-8; that is, eight on the top, nine below, and so on to the bottom of the box. Custom also requires that each row be arranged from the darkest wrapper on the left to the lightest on the right.

Any good merchant will allow you to open the box to examine its contents. Check first for consistency of color. If there is a significant difference and the box has been opened it could be that there has been a failure in the quality-control process in the packing, or that some of the cigars have been switched from a different box. Ask to have a look at another box.

The visual inspection should also focus on the spiral of the wrapper leaf. It ought to be in the same direction for all the cigars. Next, if possible, smell and feel them, looking for the signs of freshness and good construction described earlier.

When buying cigars by the box you would be wise to keep in mind that some cigar merchandisers may emphasize the packaging over the contents. Fancy boxes have been part of the attraction of cigars for a hundred and fifty years. Collecting cigar boxes can be as feverish as the pursuit of other antiques (see chapter 8). But elaborate boxes can add greatly to the overall cost of cigars. Those that come in polished and beveled cedar or mahogany boxes can be very expensive. Aluminum or glass tubes can also add to the price.

One thing is clear about buying cigars by the box: The purchaser has obviously made a commitment to smoking cigars. But acquiring them in quantity carries with it the challenge of proper storage of these prizes until they can be enjoyed.

To do that, you will want another kind of box.

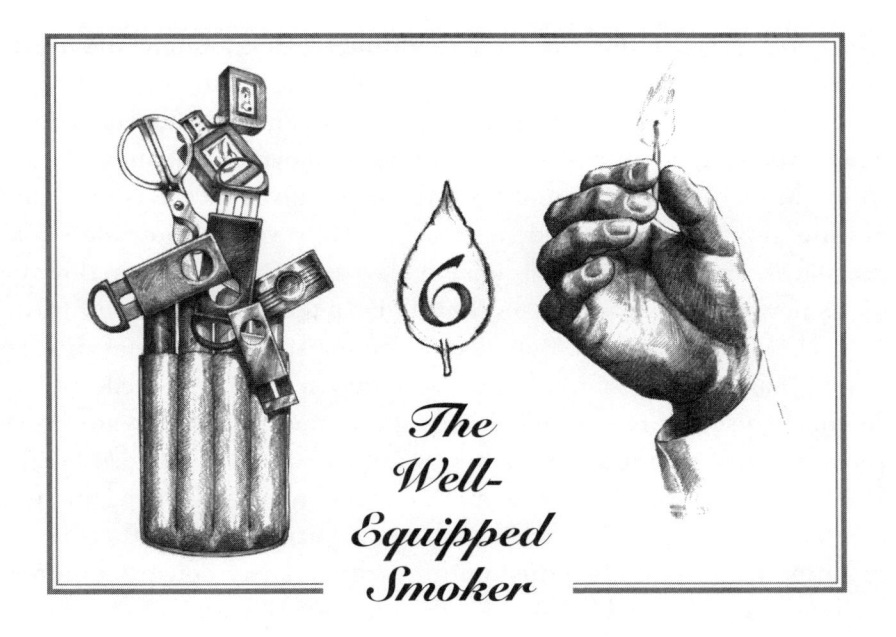

The Well-Equipped Smoker

A GOOD HUMIDOR IS NOT JUST ANOTHER BOX.
—Zino Davidoff

Humidors

"Shoddiness can be found easily, in quantity: The road is smooth and it lies close by," declared Winston Churchill to embattled Britons as they stood alone in the early years of World War II, "but in front of excellence the immortal gods have put sweat, and long and steep is the way out."

The quotation appears on the cover of a brochure put out by the Boston Cigar Cutter Company, one of many firms devoted to the manufacture of an array of devices, equipment, and gizmos to aid in the smoking and enjoyment of cigars.

Churchill's theme was echoed by cigar researcher Michael Frank. In a magazine article on how to keep cigars as fresh as possible he wrote that because they are an agricultural product, "some amount of sweat and cash must be spent" to correctly preserve them.

Indeed, copious amounts of perspiration and troves of cash have been expended in pursuit of the utmost enjoyment of cigars since Columbus's worthy seamen discovered the natives of the New World puffing away with such evident pleasure. However, the intruders into the places where tobacco abounded had to deal with a problem that the locals never needed to confront: how to keep the wonderful stuff fresh.

The issue is the maintenance of the moisture of the leaf in such a state that it can be smoked and not merely set on fire. Dried-out leaf cannot be used. If not stored at the right temperature there are worse consequences. Too much heat brings out the dreaded tobacco beetle. Only a long process of experimentation in techniques of curing and fermentation, as well as in packing and transporting, eventually resulted in a product that can be relied on for consistency of construction and freshness. But they still must be stored in the right way.

The solution is a box. But not just any one will do. Because of the preservative qualities of Spanish cedar, so abundant in the Cuban countryside, that wood became the cigar industry's hallmark for delivering as fresh a smoke as possible. The next question for the consumer was that of keeping the cigar in the same state of freshness in home or office. While the original box sufficed, and although, as will be seen, cigar box decorations approached art, the run-of-the-mill box usually did not lend itself to the decor of home or office. Or one's status.

What those who bought their cigars in bulk desired was an effective means of keeping them as fresh as possible, and within easy reach. Sherlock Holmes's solution was to pile his supply of cigars between his chair and the fireplace—in a coal scuttle.

A better idea is the humidor. It is, of course, still a box. But the difference is in the addition of woodworking craftsmanship, even artistry, to the practical necessity of storage in a way to keep the contents fresh. A strictly utilitarian container became a highly attractive ornament as well, and, in some instances, a room furnishing.

"Like a cigar, a well-built humidor enhances many experiences, rewards its owner with keen and lasting memories, and provides him with many pleasures," writes Michael Frank. "This isn't simple, because a humidor should re-create the tropical or semitropical environment in which most tobacco is grown."

Customarily made of walnut, mahogany, or rosewood on the exterior, the best humidors range in price from a couple of hundred to thousands of dollars and store as few as twenty-five and as many as five hundred cigars. The chief difference between them and ordinary cigar boxes is the installation of a hygrometer to regulate the inside humidity. A relatively modern innovation, it replaced the early attempts at humidity control that had included placing in a cigar box an apple core, a sponge, or a wet cloth. The recommended humidity is 70 to 72 percent, with a temperature of 68 to 70 degrees F. To accomplish this, use a small sponge containing plain water or special chemical compounds, or perhaps a small bottle. Whatever the device, it must be examined on a regular basis to make certain it contains sufficient fluid to do the job.

Many styles of humidors also are equipped with vertical separators to keep cigars neatly stacked. Others offer trays. What is most important, however, is how well it has been put together. Joinings of the wood should be perfectly squared and fitted with no evidence of gaps or signs of glue. The preferred inside wood is still cedar. The interior must not be varnished. The lid should be heavy and sturdy enough to close snugly without a lock.

Some premium humidors in the 1990s, with capacities ranging from twenty-five to five hundred, follow on the next page.

Brand/maker/no.	Price
Club Imports/30*	$420
Davidoff	
No. 3/75	$1400
No. 800 Red Mahogany/110	$1600
Dunhill Mahogany 25	$630
Nat Sherman	
25	$375–$575
50	$685
100	$975
500	$4750
Savinelli/150	$250
Zino	
Macassar GM/150	$1225
Plexi-Acrylic/25–50	$165

*Numbers indicate quantity of cigars held.

Some humidors have an inner box of cedar and the exterior made of clear or smoked acrylic. For example, Hinds Brothers Tobacco Ltd. of Winnipeg, Canada, markets its Reserve Collection in three sizes. The 18" x 12" x 8" Reserve I holds up to 100 double-Corona-sized cigars (retail price in US $398); Reserve II accommodates up to 75 Churchills (16" x 10" x 6" at $338); and the Reserve III (10" x 8" x 6") at $268 holds up to 50 Coronas.

Should cost put a humidor's solution to home/office storage problem out of reach, the Thompson Cigar Company of Tampa, Florida, in a leaflet titled "A Connoisseur's Guide to Cigar Smoking Pleasure," proposes a means of storage available to anyone: "You may also store your cigars in a refrigerator, provided the cellophane wrapping around the box is unbroken. If broken, the cigars may tend to absorb food odors. Also, a frost-free refrigerator will tend to draw moisture from cigars if the wrap is broken."

No one has ever recommended stashing cigars in the freezer.

Should you have the finances to afford the top of the line in cigar storage you can put in an order for a custom-made Nat Sherman Ultimate Humidor. In a cabinet of genuine, full-grained mahogany are shelves or trays of Spanish cedar. Ten drawers will accommodate about one thousand cigars. They are moisturized by means of a one-gallon reserve of distilled water. A 50,000-hour fan motor drives the cool moisture down through a tube to the bottom of the humidor. All this is monitored electronically.

For those seeking a sturdy storage chest without the premium price, the J-R Tobacco Company of America's catalog offers a $20 surplus army .50-caliber ammunition box lined with Honduran cedar and outfitted with a "velcro mounted, teensy-weensie removable humidifying device," along with complete suggestions for "proper usage and identification labels so you won't have to keep opening boxes every week to remember exactly what cigar you stored, and when you stored it!"

Celebrating his 71st birthday in 1945, former British Prime Minister Winston Churchill paused on his way to Parliament to pose for a photo with his wife Clementine, grandson Winston, and his favorite Dunhill El Tovador Selection No. 60. After a German bombing raid on London during the second world war, Churchill's tobacconist telephoned him with assurances that his cigars had come through the attack safely.

Alfred Dunhill Archive Collection

Pocket cigar holders are available in leather (shown), metal and plastic. They vary in holding capacity from two to six and are available in the most popular lengths and ring-gauges.

Courtesy of Nat Sherman

The boxes are also advertised as providing certainty that "if somebody breaks into your house they won't take your priceless cigars, cause they'll think the boxes just contain some stinky old machine gun bullets."

Those cigar smokers with sufficient finances and ample room in home or office to store considerably more than a few boxes of favorite brands and styles can attain a sublime level by creating a special climate-controlled space especially for them. It may be a closet tailored to the needs of storage, or an entire room. It may even achieve the grandeur found in wine cellars.

Others follow the example of Winston Churchill and confine their supply to the care and keeping of their tobacconist. For example, Nat Sherman's famous cigar emporium on Fifth Avenue in New York City advises customers who have found a particularly cherished variety, "We will be glad to accept your order for an increased quantity of these cigars which we will then keep in our scientifically controlled humidors, marked (of course) with your name and personal reserve label. These cigars can be shipped to you on a subscription basis or on call as you desire. If you like, you can visit the club floor humidor and help yourself to your 'stash.'"

The downside of storing your cigars in a tobacconist's humidor is that your smokes will be available to you only when the shop is open. And, like Churchill, watch out for air raids!

While a humidor is ideal for storing cigars at home or in the office, for the best care and handling of cigars while on the move a different system is a must.

The Cigar Case

The earliest mention of a smoker carrying cigars in a case appears in a work by Jean Labat, a Catholic missionary in the West Indies. Writing in 1693, he made note of "Negroes and Indians" carrying their *cigales* (Spanish for "locusts") in little pouches made of leather.

In the intervening centuries, toting a small supply of cigars while on the move has become considerably more practical, trustworthy, and elegant. Modern cases, also called travel humidors, come in an array of sizes and styles and, of course, prices. Some have moisture regulators. Prices can run into hundreds of dollars. The classiest can cost a thousand or more. The difference between them and humidors for home and office is that these boxes are built to withstand the rigors of being transported in suitcases. The best can be gotten from such premier tobacco merchants as Davidoff, Dunhill, Michel Perrenoud International, and Nat Sherman, and fine department stores such as Harrods in London.

The most widely used method of carrying cigars is the pocket case. Multifingered cases keep each cigar separate from its companions. Some have moisture regulators and some don't. They can be made of leather, plastic, or metal and feature removable tops (tubular) or lids that remain attached when open (telescopic). Size, capacity, and price are related to length and ring gauge of the cigar. They also run the gamut of material, style, and price, as illustrated by those made by Ashton and sold by Holt's of Philadelphia. The firm's mail-order catalog for 1995 offered the cases listed on next page in a choice of black or brown and goatskin or pigskin.

TUBULAR:

Type/size/capacity		Price(s)
Lonsdale or Corona up to 63/4 x 44	(2)	140
	(3)	165
	(4)	185
Robusto up to 51/2 x 52	(2)	160
	(3)	190
	(4)	220
Pyramid up to 6 x 54	(2)	180
	(3)	250
	(4)	325
Corona Gorda or Churchill up 63/4 x 54	(2)	160
	(3)	180
	(4)	200
Double Corona up to 81/2 x 52	(1)	130
	(2)	165
	(3)	200
	(4)	230

TELESCOPIC:

Type/size/capacity		Price(s)
Robusto up to 6 x 52	(2)	140
	(3)	165
	(4)	190
Any length up to 48 ring	(2)	130
	(3)	140
	(4)	155
	(5)	165

OTHER EXAMPLES:

Brand/material/capacity	Price	Source
Agme Swiss, pigskin (4)	50	Agme, Switzerland
Ashton, goatskin (2)	155	Holt's, Phildelphia
D. Marshall, calf (3)	150	Dunhill of London
Davidoff, wood tube (1)	100	Davidoff, Geneva
Holt's		
President, black (3)	54	Holt's, Philadelphia
Robusto, pigskin (3)	34	
Toro, pigskin (3)	50	
Nat Sherman		
Silver (1)	45	Nat Sherman,
(2)	55	New York
(3)	65	
Leather(2)	35	
(3) smooth finish	27.50	
(3) Robusto size	28	
(3) 50 ring	37.50	
Black Moroccan (3)	120	
Black Lizard (2)	150	
Brown Lizard (3)	160	
Black Crocodile (2)	485	

Cutters

Nature provides the most readily available means of opening the head of a cigar—teeth. Although at some time or other probably every cigar smoker has had to incise the business end of a smoke by biting, it is not the ideal way to do so. A cutter is best for slicing the head of a cigar. It may be no more exotic than a pocketknife. Or it can be a tool made for the purpose in the form of a small scissors or a device with a name that is rather dreadful in the image it evokes—a guillotine. With this apparatus, the head of the cigar is inserted through a hole and then chopped off with the quick action of a blade.

As in all aspects of cigar smoking, there are varieties and prices to suit every taste and purse.

Pocket-sized scissor-style cutters are among the popular devices for preparing the head of a cigar.

Some examples:

Davidoff

cutter, $47.50

steel scissors, $300

Dunhill

Guillotine, silver plated, $350

gold plated, $485

cutter with built-in electric lighter, $59.95

Nat Sherman

Guillotine:

Gold-plated stainless steel, square, $250

Satin finish stainless steel, round, $160

Satin finish stainless steel, square, $250

Sterling silver diamond pattern, square, $315

Silver-plated diamond, rectangle, $215

Silver-plated, hexagon, $215

Tortoise shell, octagon, $450

Scissors:

Gold tone pocket, $52

Chrome pocket, $48

Satin finish stainless steel, $200

Rowenta, chrome-plated steel

with quartz-electronic lighter, $120

Zino Davidoff, large ring, $45

Holt's

Pocket guillotine, chrome, $16

Pocket scissors, nickel, gold, steel, $48

Pocket spring-action guillotine, nickel, $22

square spring, large ring, gold, chrome, $44

Table scissors, nickel, gold, steel, $55

Cigar guillotines are also made to be non-portable. Designed to stand on a table or a desktop, they can be quite handsome, as well as intricate. A prime example is the Boston Cigar Cutter Company's "Classic Cutter." Billed by the maker as "a hardwood-and-Sheffield-steel work of art that is also a precision instrument of superb quality," the machine features a cork base and a spring-loaded, precision rotary cutter. The device is available in whatever ring the buyer prefers (small, large, or both) with assurances that the machine "effortlessly produces a perfectly sheared 'cat's-eye' cut that provides maximum draw with minimal invasive damage to the head of your cigar." A cat's-eye cut differs from a flat or V-cut in that it trims close to the edge and makes a deeper cut in the middle.

A convenient form of cutter is the hand-held guillotine, as in this example from the Nat Sherman collection. Other guillotines are much larger and designed for use in the home or office. Courtesy of Nat Sherman

To personalize the device the company offers an optional monogram plate, a choice of left- or right-handed, and a menu of selections in wood finish and metal trim. Resharpening is also offered. Prices start at around $400.

Rather than use a cutter, some smokers choose to ready their cigars for smoking by poking a hole with a punch. This technique accomplishes the purpose; however, it carries with it the risk of drilling the hole too deeply, thereby causing the tobacco to burn quickly and hot. Nat Sherman's 1995 catalog prices punches at $60 (smooth finish) and $75 (hammered). Some pipe smokers who also enjoy the occasional cigar have been known to use the poking part of their pipe-cleaning tool as a cigar punch.

Should you decide to store your cigars in the surplus ammo boxes offered in the J-R catalog, you may wish to nip those cigars with a cutter made from an actual .44 magnum bullet. Shipped with gift box and velour carrying pouch, it recently was advertised in Holt's catalog at $12.95.

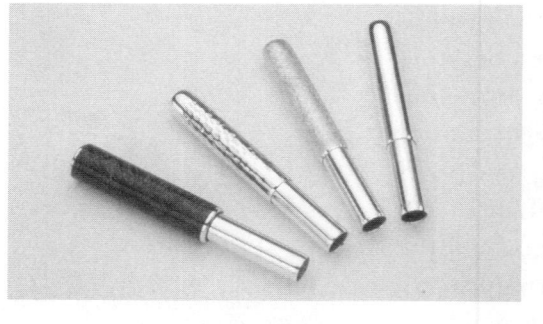

A popular alternative to cutters as a means of opening the head of a cigar is the punch. These stainless-steel examples are marketed by Nat Sherman. Courtesy of Nat Sherman

What about lighting up? Should it be by lighter or by match?

Lighters, Etc.

Again, how a cigar is lighted is a matter of an individual's preference, based on experience, as is the price one is willing to pay for a lighter. Disposable ones are available cheaply almost everywhere. Better-made and more elegant lighters cost accordingly.

Some examples:

Colibri

   Quantum Bean, $95

   Quantum Guard, $65

   Electro-quartz, $55

Dunhill

   Black lacquer finish, $485

   Gold tone bamboo, $395

Montecristo

   Gold-plated lighter, $250

Peterson's

   Chantilly, $30.95

   Chelsea, $28.95

   Dart, $39.95

   La Crosse, $50

If any lighter has earned a place in American history, it is the Zippo. Inspired to invent an inexpensive but always reliable lighter, George Blaisdell in 1932 came up with a design in which a flip-top cover could be tilted back and the flicking of a flint wheel could be achieved with one hand. Featuring a windshield to surround flint and wick and compact enough to fit snugly in the hand, it was made of brass with a chromium finish and priced at $1.95. But it was not until World War II that "Zippo" would become synonymous with "lighter." Because of superb functionality, durability, reliability, and a reputation for being as "windproof" as advertised, the Zippo was the ideal lighter to slip into the pocket of a uniform and carry off to war. Millions of GIs lit cigarettes and cigars with them from training camp to foxhole and continued to use them after mustering out, making the Zippo the world's most popular lighter among men.

Extolling the virtues of the lighter in an article in *CIGAR Aficionado* in December 1993, Rene Chun saw "something inherently masculine about a Zippo lighter," from its clean-cut lines and utilitarianism to the "*ping* sound" when it is opened that "strikes a chord in the hearts of all men."

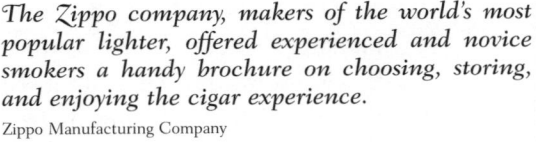

The Zippo company, makers of the world's most popular lighter, offered experienced and novice smokers a handy brochure on choosing, storing, and enjoying the cigar experience.
Zippo Manufacturing Company

While the Zippo remains reliable and durable and maintains its popularity, its use as a cigar lighter carries with it the risk that its petroleum-based fluid will taint the taste of the cigar. However, the firm in a small brochure aimed at the cigar smoker argues that "any source of flame will impart a taste to the cigar if the proper lighting method is not observed," then describes the right way to light up, while pointing out that if you use your Zippo properly, all fuel smells will dissipate before the cigar is lit.

Setting the fuel-taste issue aside, the Zippo rates high as a reliable, inexpensive, nondisposable lighter. One with a brush chrome finish costs $12.95 and the polished chrome is a dollar more. A black matte finish with full-color American flag ("Old Glory," model No. 2180G) is $14.95. The lighters now are highly collectible, so much so that the manufacturer publishes "The Zippo Lighter Collectors Guide," which lists every style and model between 1932 and the present. (See "The Cigar Smoker's Source Guide" for the address, along with a listing of lighter-collecting clubs.)

As to matches for cigar lighting, wooden ones are better than paper because they burn longer. Pocket-sized boxes are generally available wherever cigars are sold. Many fine restaurants, despite the inroads of the smoke police, employ them as advertising and heap them in bowls next to the door. Wise smokers should help themselves and stock up, for there is no telling when the antismoking movement may fix its sights on the lowly match as a tool of Satan to be banished from society.

Rosebud brand matches, made by the Universal Match Company of Minneapolis, can be found in some (not all, alas) supermarkets in packages of ten for about ninety cents, though the price of these excellent matches has risen sharply, from about three cents a box not so long ago. Dunhill sells sulphur-frees in a pocket-sized box at $3.75 per box.

Connoisseurs also have a choice of premium ashtrays. Nat Sherman's stock includes one of black stoneware with ample room for the ash and a comfortably long cradle for the cigar, at $25. Fine ashtrays can be bought in shops and stores featuring high-quality glass and crystal, as well. But this useful artifact of centuries of smoking is already becoming a rarity as restaurants and hotels, bullied by the fervent antismoking activists and new laws, have removed them from tables and rooms in many places. It may be that the ashtray also will fall victim to antitobacco militants and end up either banned altogether or classified as paraphernalia associated with an outlaw practice, much as the implements of narcotics use have been made illegal.

The same fate also may befall an item of clothing that has been through the age of tobacco a symbol of luxury and personal style—the smoking jacket. What movie attempting to depict class and taste has not included a scene in which a character has, after dinner, slipped into one of fancy silk, satin, or velvet to settle into a large wingback chair in front of a cozy fireplace with a cigar in hand and a snifter of brandy within easy reach?

The moment might be suave Laurence Olivier pining the loss of a lover or debonair William Powell as private eye Nick Charles mulling over who done it. In one Sherlock Holmes episode on PBS's *Mystery!*, Dr. Watson (Edward Hardwicke) wears a smoking jacket and a fez while explaining (for once) to Holmes (Jeremy Brett) the intricacies of their present dastardly puzzle—while smoking a cigar, of course.

For those with a bent for nostalgia and the romantic, Nat Sherman's 1995 catalog offered a re-creation of "the classic 18th Century's gentlemen's smoking jacket," along with a tasseled fez. Made in Manchester, England, with a soft velvet body and collared and cuffed with black silk, jacket and fez were available as a set at $467.50 in "regal burgundy."

Bedecked in such a manner a man can bide his time deciding which cigar to choose from the glorious temptations spread out in the humidor. With a guillotine, a lighter, an ashtray, and cognac waiting, and Mozart as accompaniment, who would not feel kinship with countless comrades down the years who discovered that in the companionship of a cigar and its beguiling smoke:

> *A magic charm in the evening calm*
> *Calls thought from mem'ry's treasure;*
> *But clear and bright in the liquid light*
> *Are the smoke-called dreams of pleasure.*

7

The Best of Company

HE SET HIS GLASS ON THE TABLE AND HELD THE BOX OF
CORONAS DEL RITZ OUT TO SPADE.
—*Dashiell Hammett*

S amuel Spade took a cigar, trimmed the end, and lighted it. Caspar Gutman was a man who would tell you right out that he was a man who liked to talk to a man who liked to talk.

That was swell, said the private detective. Would they talk about the black bird?

A moment later in Hammett's *The Maltese Falcon,* the 1929 private-eye classic that has been the touchstone for every hard-boiled yarn since, Spade blows smoke above the fat man's head in a long slanting plume and frowns thoughtfully at the ash at the tip of his cigar. Then the talking turns to a woman.

With Humphrey Bogart as Spade and the extra-portly Sydney Greenstreet as Gutman the scene unfolds even more thrillingly in the

1940 movie. And how fitting it is that their co-stars are a brace of double Coronas. Cigarettes finish too soon. Pipes are both cumbersome and not in keeping with either man's character. A discussion that ranges from a fabulous jeweled statuette of a bird to a dangerous, double-dealing woman requires something formidable, long lasting, and conducive to some serious thought, weighty business, and gentlemanly conversation.

Of course, the cigarette has enjoyed its share of dramatic moments. There is the scene in *Now, Voyager* when Paul Henreid lights two, one for himself and the other for Bette Davis. The love-wracked Bogart in *Casablanca* has a cigarette in one hand and a glass of whiskey in the other while he laments to Sam, piano player and friend, that out of all the gin joints in the world Ingrid Bergman had to walk into his. But such instances in which the cigarette is integral to the illumination of character have been few and far between. Although Bette Davis could wave a cigarette and underscore her warning to guests at a party to "fasten your seat belts, it's going to be a bumpy night," most of the time handling a cigarette has been a way to keep an actor's hands occupied. In everyday life, recourse to a cigarette has been either habitual or a method of relieving nervous tension, rather than a clue to the smoker's inner being.

This rarely pertains to a pipe, which has been stereotyped in the public's mind as symbolic of braininess, due in large measure to images of Sherlock Holmes as he tackles complicated mysteries in books, on stage, in the movies, and on television, and countless other images of men as thinkers—professors in tweedy jackets or sweaters with elbow patches; scientists of the Albert Einstein caliber; friendly family physicians making house calls; and concerned TV fathers of the stripe of Fred MacMurray in *My Three Sons*, Robert Young of *Father Knows Best*, and Hugh Beaumont as Ward Cleaver in *Leave It to Beaver*.

Nor has the subject of this book ever been put into a man's hand in literature or the visual media merely to serve as a prop. The cigar has been, and is, far more symbolic. Carrying or smoking one conveys, as noted earlier, a potent statement that can be personal, social, political, or economic. Poet John Galsworthy was right: "By the cigars they smoke, ye shall know the texture of men's souls."

Zino Davidoff writes of cigar smoking: "Sublime moments. Precious moments, and like the smoke that rises from the gray ash, fleeting but unforgettable ones."

Mentioned and quoted throughout this book, Zino Davidoff stands as a giant in the story of cigars. He is one of the few individuals whose names are associated with promoting excellence in making them and in setting high standards in their marketing. His book, *The Connoisseur's Book of the Cigar,* published in 1967, is a landmark in the literature of the cigar. And the firm he established to sell and promote cigars still bears his name and continues to thrive in Switzerland.

Born in Russia, he fell in love with cigars as a youth in his father's shop in Kiev at the time of the Russian Revolution. His book relates how one of his father's customers, one Vladimir Ulyanov, changed his name to Lenin and went on to bring Communism to Russia, while leaving behind for the Davidoffs a bill for cigars that to this day exists, stamped NOT PAID.

Sent by his father to the Americas "in order to learn something about the tobacco trade," Zino spent time in Brazil discovering "black tobacco—the tobacco of cigars." From there he went to Cuba feeling "a state of anticipation a young archeologist might for Greece or a seminarian for Rome."

"Eventually," he remembers in his book, "I knew which were the best cigars in the world—and why."

He meant Cubans, of course. But by the time he published his book that fair island and its tobacco growers had fallen under the heel of Castro-style Communism and many of its most illustrious tobacco families had fled, taking their skills elsewhere in the Americas. Yet he insists in his book that "surviving every vicissitude, a good Havana with a gold or purple band, in its wooden box with cedar shavings, encased

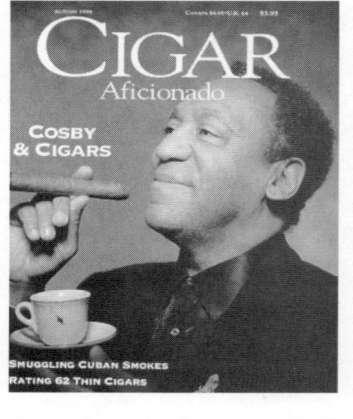

Comedian and actor Bill Cosby was featured on the cover of the Autumn 1994 issue of CIGAR Aficionado. With the renewed popularity of cigar smoking and the appearance of magazines devoted to cigars, makers of premium brands, unable to promote their products on television because of a federal ban on tobacco commercials, turned to slick advertisements in the new publications. Courtesy M. Shanken Communications, Inc.

in its baroque splendor, is still the master of the cigar world."

Among Davidoff's many contributions to the world of cigars is the humidified storage room, and he claimed to have made "the first of the humidors." In the pages of his order books one can find the names and cigar preferences of kings, dukes, millionaires, adventurers, celebrities, and even some "beautiful women," all brought together by a common bond—the cigar.

That bond continues to bring people together all over the world and from every side of life, and in increasing numbers. Between 1992 and 1995 the covers of *CIGAR Aficionado* have featured comedian Groucho Marx, comics Bill Cosby and George Burns, millionaire and boss of Consolidated Cigar Ron Perelman, conservative talk-show host Rush Limbaugh, and movie superstar Jack Nicholson. Other celebrities and prominent individuals of the 1990s counted in the ranks of cigar smokers are comedian and television pioneer Milton Berle, sports broadcaster Ahmad Rashad, actor Ben Gazzara, comedian Jim Belushi, professional football Hall-of-Famer Terry Bradshaw, film director Francis Ford Coppola, historian Arthur Schlesinger Jr., and a star of one of the decade's most popular television dramas, Dennis Franz of *NYPD Blue*.

Another television personality who considers himself a cigar lover is the host of CBS's popular *Late Show*, although David Letterman did succumb briefly to antismoking critics. They had faulted him for smoking cigars, especially when he did so on the air or was caught by the camera after a commercial break in a cloud of smoke from the cigar he had puffed in the interim. The respite from cigars lasted less than a year. Admitting to another talk-show host, Larry King, that he had resumed smoking, he said, "I missed it desperately. I missed everything about it. I like the feel, I like the smell, I like the taste."

In answer to criticism by Edgar Lichstein, chairman of the public policy board of the antismoking American Heart Association, who said Letterman ought to "set a good example" by not smoking on the air, Marvin Shanken retorted, "It's nonsense. It's a late-night program, not something for the kids. It's a program that represents the good life, and I don't know what represents the good life better than cigar smoking."

No one appears to be more in tune with the good life than John F. Kennedy Jr. The handsome son of the late president has been a frequent customer of Barclay Rex, a midtown Manhattan cigar emporium where he is reported to favor Griffin's, Davidoffs, and Larranagas. However, one of Kennedy's shopping forays impelled a newspaper gossip page to point out that the senior John F. Kennedy had "put an embargo on trade with the greatest tobacco country in the unfree world, making it a real pain in the butt—although not impossible—for cigar smokers to enjoy a good Cohiba now and again."

Young Kennedy is not the only member of the family favoring cigars. His uncle, Senator Edward (Ted) Kennedy, is rarely seen at a white-tie function in Washington, DC, without lighting up a cigar after dinner. In doing so, he is seldom alone. Among the denizens of Capitol Hill who favor a good cigar (despite the specter of "the smoke-filled room") are: Supreme Court Associate Justices Clarence Thomas and Antonin Scalia, U.S. Senators Howell Heflin and Christopher (Kit) Bond, Representative Henry Hyde, and a cohort of other congressmen from both parties. Perhaps the most public of these devotees of "the stogie" is pugnacious Congressman Jack Brooks of Texas, who did not give a damn if he was seen with a cigar in his mouth while sitting on a committee. He once warned a smoke police complainant, "Just try and get this cigar away from me."

Former Washington luminaries who light up an occasional cigar are ex–Secretary of State Alexander Haig; Bernard Nussbaum, ex-counsel to President Bill Clinton; ex–House Speaker Jim Wright; and the man who also presided from the same podium, the late Thomas P. (Tip) O'Neill. It was Tip who once advised Vice President Walter Mondale, "Enjoy the good cigars, Fritz. They're about all that damn job's good for."

Although Mondale was careful not to be seen smoking a cigar while he was antismoking Jimmy Carter's running mate in 1976, neither he nor President Ronald Reagan had any problem with their faces on the bands of cigars sold as fund-raisers on their behalf during the 1984 campaign for the White House. While Reagan was not known for smoking cigars during eight years as the country's chief executive, he smoked them in many of his cowboy movies.

The first chief executive on record who smoked cigars is also the first to reside in the executive mansion. John Adams moved into "the President's house" in 1800 (the mansion would not be formally named the White House until the administration of Teddy Roosevelt, a nonsmoker because he had asthma). Those after John Adams who favored a good cigar are James Madison, John Quincy Adams (like father, like son), Andrew Jackson, John Tyler, Zachary Taylor, Andrew Johnson, Ulysses Grant, Chester Arthur, Benjamin Harrison, William McKinley, William Howard Taft, Warren Harding, Calvin Coolidge, Herbert Hoover, John F. Kennedy, Lyndon Johnson, and Richard Nixon.

President George Bush also enjoyed cigars, as did his press secretary, Marlin Fitzwater, although both often found themselves upbraided for it by the otherwise delightful Barbara Bush.

To make matters worse in the capital, new federal laws were passed to prohibit smoking in public buildings and Senator Frank Lautenberg of New Jersey went so far as to attempt to officially declare the Senate a smoke-free zone, just as Hillary Rodham Clinton had NO SMOKING signs put up in the White House. They are enforced, except

Although Hillary Clinton imposed a "no smoking" rule at the White House, President Bill Clinton lit up a cigar in the Oval Office to celebrate the rescue of an American pilot who had been shot down over Bosnia. The Chief Executive is shown here with an unlit cigar as he golfed at the Belle Haven Country Club in Alexandria, Virginia, on February 27, 1996.
AP/Wide World Photos

on rare occasions, such as following the rescue of an American airman from hostiles.

One can only imagine the damage that might have been done to the "special relationship" between Britain and the United States if Eleanor Roosevelt, Bess Truman, or Mamie Eisenhower had had the temerity to inform Winston Churchill during his frequent visits with their husbands that he would not be allowed to light up his cherished cigars under the roof of the executive mansion. Given President Clinton's acquiescence to the ban it seems unlikely that future cigar smokers will find themselves smoking a Clinton as they do a Churchill.

Clinton's apparent schizophrenia on the issue of smoking does not go unnoticed by the Washington press corps. Reminding him he had authorized tough new regulations to keep cigarettes away from teenagers, reporters quickly pointed out his own indulgence in cigars.

This prompted a newspaper column by Jeff Greenfield in which he suggests language Clinton might have used to chastise the press for equating cigars with cigarettes.

It read, in part, "In fact, it's you people in the media who have defamed the cigar. Every time you need a villain, you put a cigar in his mouth: the blood-sucking capitalist lighting cigars with $20 bills; the rich, fat movie villains portrayed by Edward Arnold or Sydney Greenstreet; [and] the political bosses in their smoke-filled rooms—it's nothing less than group libel."

Greenfield argued that Clinton should have silenced critics with the rejoinder, "The cigar is the symbol of success; when the great Boston Celtics coach Red Auerbach would light up a cigar, that was his way of signaling when the game was won. When a man becomes a father, what does he pass out to his friends? Cigarettes? Don't be ridiculous; he hands out cigars. When someone falls just short of achieving a goal, what do we say? 'Close, but no cigar.' When that goal is finally achieved, what do we say? 'Give that man a cigar.' But do we really mean to drive every mild indulgence out of our lives? Can't we make room for the occasional marbled steak, the hot dog and beer at a ballgame, bacon and eggs for Sunday breakfast, and, yes, the after-dinner cigar?"

What the ban on smoking in the White House achieved was the removal from the State and East Room dining tables of a prized souvenir of a visit to the White House. Gone are the elegant white matchfolders embossed in gold with THE PRESIDENT'S HOUSE.

These desirable mementos also disappeared from the fleet of presidential aircraft. Undoubtedly they would have been taken off the presidential yacht as well, had Jimmy Carter's administration not sold it.

However, all is not bleak for cigar smokers in the nation's capital. They still light up and enjoy at the embassies of the cigar-producing countries of Latin America. Yet one can only wonder if the law barring smoking in U.S. government buildings would include the American embassy in Havana, Cuba, that one day surely will become a reality in the years after the demise of the Castro regime.

Meanwhile, the antismoking crusade has affected nongovernment places in Washington, as it has everywhere else. Some of the city's most famous and historic restaurants imposed smoking restrictions to the point that Washington wag Art Buchwald moaned on behalf of cigar smokers, "A man could get killed these days lighting a cigar in a restaurant."

Rebellion was inevitable.

New Yorkers with a passion for literature as well as cigars have a choice of three enterprises described in an article by Neil Graves in the *Daily News* under the headline "Saloons with a sense of humidor." Devised by Mark Grossich, Bar and Books operates on First Avenue and 50th Street, Hudson Street in Greenwich Village, and 1020 Lexington Avenue on the Upper East Side.

Trademarks are paneled walls, lush seats, subdued lighting, and wall units piled high with literary classics.

"Patrons may think they have stepped back in time into Cornelius Vanderbilt's study to share a puff with the baron," wrote Graves. The establishments offer baby boomers "a place to close a deal by day or to groove on live jazz weekend nights."

Appropriate attire is a requirement: "We've brought back the dress coat," Grossich said. "It's a return to a bygone era when that was considered the way to go."

A General Cigar subsidiary, Culbro, announced another Manhattan spa for cigar smokers. Called Club Macanudo, it opened early in 1996 at 26 East 63rd Street, the former site of the upscale Quo Vadis restaurant. Club Macanudo offers a full range of cigars, wine, scotches, port, and brandies, as well as light food, in a luxuious leather and brass atmosphere, complete with private humidors.

Also for the benefit of New York cigar smokers is a thirty-four-seat restaurant/lounge "catering to the sophisticated cigar smoker seeking the finer things in life," in the words of a press release. The Cigar Room at Trumpets is in the Grand Hyatt hotel next to Grand Central Terminal. The room was announced at a charity gala aboard the retired aircraft carrier (now a museum) USS *Intrepid*. The affair was for the benefit of the Sorvino Asthmatic Foundation, founded by actor, opera singer, restaurateur, and cigar lover Paul Sorvino. Guests enjoyed a sampler of Bolivar pre-embargo Havanas from the Nat Sherman humidor.

When asked to reconcile an event for the benefit of asthma sufferers, Sorvino, the author of a book on how to overcome asthma by using a breathing technique he developed, answers, "If you have asthma you can't smoke cigars. But I don't have asthma. I've been smoking cigars ever since I was cured."

Other new oases for New York cigar smokers are in some of the city's smartest eateries. The West 63rd Street Steakhouse, which previously closed on Monday nights when most of the theaters were dark, announced that it would open its doors on Mondays to the $150-a-year members of The Cigar Club. Another restaurant, Felix, invites cigarists to dine at $75 per head and smoke to their hearts' content.

Taking note of the burgeoning movement to accommodate cigar smokers, Michel Mariott wrote in the Style section of the *New York Times* on Sunday, November 19, 1995, "Reminiscent of scenes of Madison Avenue fantasies found in many glossy magazines these days, three old friends relaxed in butter-soft sofas and armchairs fashionably arranged in a well-appointed little refuge from the rush of midtown Manhattan. For hours, the men, handsome and crisp as new money, alternately laughed and joked and spoke seriously about their work, family, and selves. All the while, each blissfully puffed away on a premium cigar, heavily scenting the Cigar Bar of the Beekman Bar and Books, on First Avenue at 50th Street, with the heady aroma of expertly aged and spiced tobacco."

The article goes on to record that from New York to Los Angeles such cigar-friendly places are "popping up like palm trees in a no-smoking desert of shifting public tastes and manners." A case in point is the Grand Havana Room, opened in July 1995 in Beverly Hills, attracting Hollywood celebrity smokers, including Joe Mantegna, Tony Danza, Dennis Franz, Alec Baldwin, Christian Slater, Jonathan Silverman, Jason Priestley, LeVar Burton, and Billy Crystal, who pay $2000 a year and $150 a month for the privilege.

"The new cigar smokers," the *Times* points out, "have little in common with the stereotypical stogie-chomping truck drivers and fat-cat politicians of old. This new wave tends to be young (mid-20s to late-30s), better educated and very discriminating as to what cigars are smoked and where."

Although Hollywood's fresh crop of cigarists is youthful, the kings of the cigar in show business were two old-timers. The legendary come-

To mark the 80th birthday of comedian George Burns in 1977, Milton Berle provided the light for their cigars. Both comedians had started their show business careers, and the smoking of cigars, as children.
AP/Wide World Photos

dian Milton Berle, who credits reaching his eighties to almost all those years spent performing, claims he never smoked cigarettes, although he began smoking cigars at age twelve. His friend and fellow comedian, George Burns, also began as a young man and, as he reached his 100th birthday, remained a devoted cigar smoker who never went on stage without one. In a tribute to Burns and recognizing that for some reason there was a link between a cigar and great comedians, Stand-Up New York, a Manhattan club for budding comics, sponsored a competition for the up-and-coming gagsters in which the only requirement, other than being funny, was the use of a cigar in their acts.

Probably nowhere in the United States has the comeback of cigar smoking been more conspicuous than in the film capital. And why not? It is in Hollywood's movies that the image of the cigar as a symbol of success and power became indelibly impressed upon the public's consciousness. In the heyday of the gangster movie it was a rare film wiseguy (Edward G. Robinson, Edward Arnold, Sydney Greenstreet, James Cagney, Humphrey Bogart, among others) who did not smoke a big black cigar in at least one scene. And the off-screen movers and shakers—the movie moguls (Jack L. Warner, Darryl F. Zanuck, Harry Cohn)—were hardly ever seen without formidable black Havanas.

While the era of such all-powerful studio titans has long passed, their modern equivalents stand solidly in the motion picture business, cigars in hand, in the form of independent superstars, producers, directors, and agents. At the top of Tinseltown's A-list in 1995 stood Arnold Schwarzenegger, Sylvester Stallone, Bruce Willis, and Tom Selleck in the superstar category; superagents Lou Pitt, Robert Bookman, and Fred Specktor; producer Andrew Bergman; and the directors Sydney Pollack and Francis Ford Coppola.

It was Coppola who united the image of the cigar-smoking Hollywood bigshot with his counterpart in organized crime in his classic gangland epic *The Godfather*. Sent out to Hollywood by mob boss

Vito Corleone to "make an offer he can't refuse" to a surly movie producer with a passion for thoroughbred racehorses, Robert Duvall as the family adviser and John Marley as the producer have after-dinner cigars while talking business. Unwisely, the producer refuses the offer. The gory scene that follows gives new meaning to "getting ahead" in the movies.

A real Hollywood mobster who enjoyed a good cigar became a pal of another cigar-smoking film tough guy, George Raft. Then Benjamin (Bugsy) Siegel went on to be the godfather of another mecca for cigars, the Nevada desert gambling oasis of Las Vegas. Unfortunately the brainstorm of this transplanted New York gangster led to Bugsy's invention of the practice of skimming the profits, for which his gangland buddies paid him off with a fusillade of bullets while he lounged on the sofa in the parlor of his girlfriend, Virgina Hill.

While Bugsy was not blasted to Kingdom Come with a stogy in his mitt, mob boss Paul Gigante was. The cigar was still there as the coroner walked into the garden dining area behind Umberto's Clam House in New York's Little Italy to cart away the remains. Anyone riffling through the photo morgues of New York's tabloid newspapers can find scores of pictures of wiseguys of past and present in which the center of attraction was snapped with a cigar in hand or mouth, from the Roaring Twenties' Gerald Chapman (the first man to be labeled Public Enemy No. 1) to 1930s godfathers Lucky Luciano and Al Capone, and the 1990s' "Teflon Don," the dapper John Gotti.

The most famous cigar-smoking gangbuster was G-man Melvin Purvis of the FBI. Personally ordered by J. Edgar Hoover to round up the most-wanted hoodlums of the 1930s, Purvis first set his sights on Pretty Boy Floyd. When the baby-faced gangster was gunned down by federal agents in a cornfield, Purvis stood next to the body and celebrated the occasion by calmly lighting a stogy. A cigar also played a role in Purvis's triumph over the decade's biggest name in crime. Informed that John Dillinger would be attending a movie at the Biograph Theater in Chicago, Purvis told his band of crimebusters that his signal to them to swoop down on the target and make an arrest would be the lighting of his cigar. But when the fateful moment arrived, Purvis was so excited and nervous that he couldn't get it lit. No matter. Merely putting the cigar up to his mouth sent the G-men into action. Dillinger fell dead in a burst of gunfire.

The Depression era's most famous female bandit also enjoyed a cigar now and then. One of the most sensational photographs of Bonnie Parker shows her with a cigar-holding hand up to her lips and a revolver in the other. The shot was re-created in the movie *Bonnie and Clyde,* starring Faye Dunaway as Bonnie and Warren Beatty as Clyde Barrow, both of whom smoked cigars.

Another woman named Parker (Dorothy) was a writer in the 1930s. One of the most acidly witty members of the "smart set" whose lunches at New York's Algonquin Hotel became immortalized as the Round Table, Dotty was observed enjoying an occasional small cigar even before she went Hollywood. Were she around today she would have no trouble fitting in with the fresh female faces who take advantage of the Grand Havana Room in the film capital, as well as the three Bar and Books in New York.

"Women come in and ask what's a good starter cigar," notes Bar and Books owner Grossich, who has held cigar seminars for women. "As we say: Panatelas are not just for fellas."

Certainly one of the interesting aspects of the comeback of the cigar in the 1990s is the willingness (even eagerness) of some women to enter the ranks of smokers. So pronounced has the movement of women into a predominantly masculine domain become that the *New York Times* felt compelled to take notice. Its "Here Now" column of August 27, 1995, bore the headline:

Stogies, a Gal's Best Friend

It begins: "The back room of the Monkey Bar was thick with spirals of smoke from 120 cigars. A guys-only, deal-clinching dinner? Not at all. In fact, barely a man was in sight."

The invitations to the $95-a-ticket event declared that it would be an evening "dedicated to women of the '90s!" Similar to the "Big Smoke" and other convocations of serious cigar smokers, it was sponsored by purveyors of premium cigars, such as Davidoff of Geneva, and offered as accompaniment superior drinks and fine cuisine (seared striped bass and roast guinea hen).

The women who filled the trendy Upper East Side restaurant with smoke were successful financially. A printing executive from New Jersey, asked about the steep costs of a night of good cigars, shrugged: "I pay more than that for a skirt," she said.

Questioned as to why she smoked, another blew a column of smoke and answered with a smile, "It's one of the greatest pleasures in life."

In making that assertion she was not, in fact, proclaiming a sudden discovery by women. They had been taking to tobacco in the form of cigars in the middle of the nineteenth century. A style of cigar called "queens" was made especially for women. Diminutive in length and girth, some were fitted with a straw mouthpiece. Earlier literary references to women who smoked go back to the 1600s, although the preferred method was more likely to be the pipe rather than a cigar. In 1665 no more distinguished a person than the Reverend Giles Moore, Rector of Horsted Keynes, Sussex, made a note in his account book that he had expended three pence for "Tobacco for my wyfe."

On September 21, 1710, Jonathan Swift, author of *Gulliver's Travels,* wrote to a friend, "I have the finest piece of Brazil tobacco for Mrs. Dingley that ever was born."

In November he wrote directly to her: "I have made Delaval [a companion of Swift] promise to send me some Brazil tobacco from Portugal for you, Madam Dingley."

The cargo list of a ship carrying Quaker women from England to Philadelphia in 1756 notes a trunk containing "balm, sage, summer

Savoury, horehound, Tobacco, and Oranges."

A hundred and fifty years later a Scotsman on a train asked a woman who sat opposite him in the compartment if she objected to him smoking. "Na, na, laddie," she replied. "I've come in here for a smoke ma'self."

Visiting Switzerland in 1846, Charles Dickens detailed his expectation of an affable evening of conversation in a hotel with his daughters and "an American lady" and her daughter of sixteen. He notes an employee of the hotel "brought out a cigar-box, and gave me a cigar, which would quell an elephant in six whiffs."

He continues:

> When I lighted my cigar, [American] daughter lighted hers at mine; leaned against the mantelpiece, laughed and talked, and smoked, in the most gentlemanly manner I ever beheld. . . . American lady immediately lighted hers; and in five minutes the room was a cloud of smoke. . . . But even this was not all. For presently two Frenchmen came in, with whom the American lady, daughter sat down to whist. The Frenchmen smoked of course, and daughter played for the next hour or two with a cigar continually in her mouth—never out of it. She certainly smoked six or eight.

The author who would give the world *Oliver Twist, David Copperfield,* and *Tale of Two Cities* was shocked.

In 1851 the English magazine *Punch* had a drawing captioned "A Quiet Smoke" that depicts five women in short wide skirts in a tobacconist's shop. Two are puffing cigars.

The woman writer with the male pseudonym of George Sand asserted in 1867, "A cigar numbs sorrows and fills the solitary hours with a million gracious images."

Although history is rife with women who adopted a contrary view, such as the monarch who reigned during the lives of Dickens and

The caption of this 1877 woodcut in Illustrated Weekly *noted that "a lady determines to enjoy her rights" by taking a seat beside her husband in the recent innovation of the smoking car of a train and joining him "in puffing a Havana cigar."* Courtesy of New York Public Library

Sand, their disdain for the aroma of cigars was not shared by writer Kate A. Carrington. In *The Scent of a Good Cigar* she finds the smell to be something sweeter than the jasmine scent and more potent in power than orange or musk.

    The ode continues:

> *I am all alone in my quiet room,*
> *And the windows are open wide and free*

To let in the south wind's kiss for me,
While I rock in the softly gathering gloom,
And that subtle fragrance steals.
Just as a loving, tender hand
Will sometimes steal in yours,
It softly comes through the open doors,
And memory wakes at its command,—
The scent of that good cigar.

Some cynical observers of societal norms and countertrends find in cigar smoking by the women of the 1990s another attempt to drive a feminist wedge into one of the few areas of modern living that still hangs out a MEN ONLY sign. These commentators view a cigar in the hand of today's woman in the same light in which another generation looked upon women wearing trousers and toting briefcases while they "invaded" that most hallowed place in the world of successful men, the corporate boardroom.

Yet, if a cigar could be the symbol of success for a man, surely a woman ought to be allowed to claim, as did the unknown author of the following:

I owe to smoking, more or less,
Through life the whole of my success;
With my cigar I'm sage and wise,—
Without, I'm dull as cloudy skies.
When smoking, all my ideas soar,
When not, they sink upon the floor.
The greatest men have all been smokers,
And so were all the greatest jokers.

Historically, although most women who decided to smoke chose cigarettes, the vast majority of their sex—as well as overwhelming numbers of men—disapproved of women smoking. But at least one English cleric, in a lecture he gave at Harvard University in 1913, in a time when smoking by women was about to become all the rage, was able to report that many women in his home country "who are well thought of, smoke."

He went on to express a view that would appear to explain the taking up of the cigar by women more than eighty years later. He preached:

> **I do not attempt to enter into the ethical part of this matter, but this much I say: If men find it such a pleasure to smoke, why shouldn't women? There are many colors in the rainbow; so there are many tastes in people. What may be a pleasure to men may be given to women. When we find women smoking, as they do in some branches of society today, the mere pleasure of that habit must be accepted as belonging to both sexes.**

Should there ever be a Smoking Hall of Fame, we believe Bishop Boyd-Carpenter deserves a plaque.

With no significance to the order in which their names appear, and aware that others might place different people on this roster, we also respectfully nominate:

Paul Auster Mastermind behind the 1995 "sleeper" movie *Smoke,* glorifying both the atmosphere and the customers in a corner cigar store in Brooklyn; shares the honor with the film's stars (Harvey Keitel, William Hurt, Stockard Channing) and the supporting players.

Theodore de Banville A French poet (1823–1891), he predicted the fad of cigarette smoking would not last because smoking cigars was more practical.

Milton Berle "Mr. Television." His first cigar, bought at the age of twelve, cost him twelve cents.

Gustave Bock From Holland, he was among the first Europeans to cultivate tobacco in Cuba. He also penned *Art of Smoking the Cigar*. Inventor of the cigar band.

Pierce Brosnan When television's "Remington Steele" inherited the role of James Bond in the movies he did so with all the panache of previous 007s and with all the Bondish accoutrements—fast cars, wickedly ingenious defensive devices designed by Q, gorgeous, enticing women, and a steady supply of his favorite Havanas.

George Burns Second only to Groucho Marx in fostering the cigar while making the world laugh. A NO SMOKING sign in a Las Vegas hotel where Burns frequently appeared advised that the ban applied only to anyone under the age of ninety-five.

Lord Byron The first poet to write an ode to the cigar.

Al Capone The top mobster in Chicago during the bootleg era, "Scarface" is the only criminal ever to have a cigar named after him—a German-made cigarillo.

Charles Chaplin "The Little Tramp" earned enough in the silent movies to keep himself supplied with the best of everything, which always included cigars.

Francois-Auguste-René de Chateaubriand An aficionado as of 1812, he also lent his name to a steak that will always be a fitting prelude to a fine cigar.

Winston Churchill Kept England and the world safe for cigars.

Henry Clay The great pre–Civil War statesman and presumably the namesake of the cigar.

Columbo Played on television by Peter Falk, this rumpled fictional lieutenant of the Los Angeles Police Department's homicide division smoked small and evidently cheap brands and constantly found himself chided by the housekeepers and butlers of his rich and famous sus-

pects for scattering ashes in their posh homes.

Howard Cosell Sports broadcaster. He was a legend in his own mind before becoming one in his trade. Though wealthy by way of generous contracts offered by his network, he was never ashamed to bum a cigar from a colleague.

Edgar M. Cullman Sr. Chairman, Culbro Corporation, parent of General Cigar, maker of Macanudo, Partagas, Garcia y Vega, and other popular brands.

The former King of England, Edward, the Duke of Windsor, a connoisseur of Havana cigars, personally inspected the Cuban factory that produced his favorite brand in 1950. Alfred Dunhill Archive Collection

Zino Davidoff The patriarch of Cuban cigars referred to himself in his book as the proprietor of "a unique shop" in Geneva.

Antoine Delpierre French privateer, he once captured an entire shipload of Dutch cigars and handed them out to the citizens of Boulogne.

Don Juan The story goes that he met the Devil by the river Guadalquivir and asked the Prince of Hell for a light for his cigar.

Raoul Dufy A great but hard-up artist (aren't they all?), he often swapped his paintings for cigars.

Duke of Windsor He gave up the throne of England for the woman he loved, but he smoked cigars to the end of his life.

Alfred Dunhill Davidoff called him "the greatest name in cigars in the

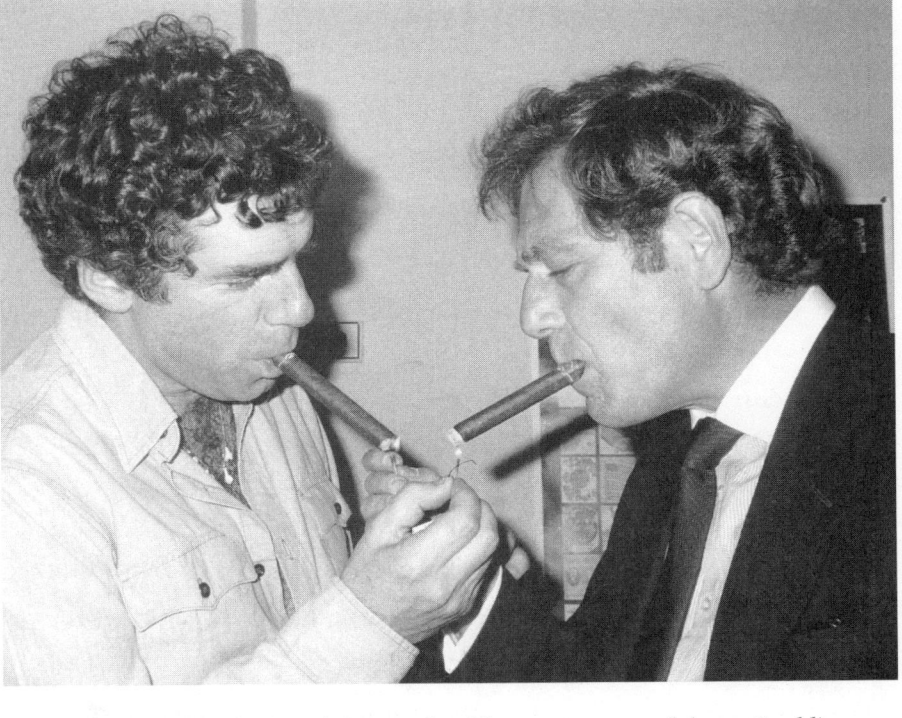

Actors Elliott Gould (L) and George Segal lit up cigars to celebrate Gould's opening night performance of "The Guys in the Truck" in June 1983. UPI/Corbis-Bettmann

English-speaking world." It appears on the façades of some of the finest emporiums of premium tobacco in the world; author of *The Gentle Art of Smoking*.

Edward VII Patient but suffering son of Queen Victoria, he returned cigars to the royal court with one of the happiest permissions in history: "Gentlemen, you may smoke." King Edward cigars proved as popular as he was.

Jake Elwell Literary agent without whom the authors of this book could not have produced it.

Farouk Despised, obese dictator of Egypt. Deposed by Nasser in the 1950s, he made a dash for exile in Europe, taking with him a trove of cigars that weighed more than he did.

Sigmund Freud The father of psychoanalysis and a devotee of the cigar advised those who saw the cigar as a phallic symbol, "Sometimes a cigar is just a cigar."

Arturo Fuente Patriarch of the cigar-making family.

Gallo Garcia Author of a treaty issued by Fulgencio Batista that permitted export of Havana cigars.

John Glenn Astronaut and U.S. Senator, he was awarded his weight in Cuban cigars after his history-making space flight in the Kennedy years.

Ulysses S. Grant Civil War general and President of the United States whose passion for cigars was equaled only by his love of the bottle.

Graham Greene Famed author of thrillers, he managed to write *Our Man in Havana* without mentioning cigars.

Tony Guida New York television news anchorman and reporter. Often found at cigar events in the Big Apple.

Bryant Gumbel Host of the morning TV news program *Today,* smoked regularly on the set, but not on camera.

Ernest Hemingway Author and namesake of a line of Fuènte cigars, famed and studied for his lean, crisp language. If you asked a Hemingway character how he liked the cigar he was smoking, he would most likely reply, "The cigar is fine."

James Jones Novelist whose *From Here to Eternity* made him the king of writers about World War II and rich enough to buy all the Havanas he wanted.

James Earl Jones Deep-voiced actor who portrayed the cigar-smoking

After President John F. Kennedy officially opened the 1962 baseball season by throwing out the first ball at DC Stadium in Washington, he settled back with a favored H. Upmann Havana. The game ended with a four-to-one win by the Washington Senators over the Detroit Tigers. A year later, in the aftermath of the Cuban Missile Crisis, Kennedy imposed the embargo on imports of Cuban cigars, but not until he ordered press secretary Pierre Salinger to lay in a White House supply of a thousand Upmanns. UPI/Corbis-Bettmann

prizefighter in *The Great White Hope,* the Broadway and film versions of the life of heavyweight Jack Jefferson. Also provided the voice of Darth Vader in the *Star Wars* movies. That Lord Vader could be a cigar smoker in that black helmet seems very unlikely.

Rudyard Kipling Author of "A good cigar is a smoke," the most quoted line in the literature of cigars and one of four listed in Bartlett's book of familiar quotations. The others: John Galsworthy on knowing a man's soul by the cigar he smokes; Vice President Marshall's wish for

The one, the only, Groucho. The cigar was as much a part of Groucho Marx's image on stage and screen as his mustache and low-slung walk. When a woman told him on his TV quiz show, You Bet Your Life, *that she had nine kids because she liked her husband, Groucho retorted, "I like a cigar, too, but every once in a while I take it out of my mouth."* Courtesy of New York Public Library.

a good five-center; Algonquin Round Table wit Franklin P. Adams's retort to Marshall:

> *The rich man has his motor car,*
> *His country and town estate,*
> *He smokes a fifty-cent cigar*
> *And jeers at Fate.*

And poet Harry Dacre's:

> *And all the world's atangle and ajar,*
> *I meditate on interstellar spaces*
> *And smoke a mild cigar.*

Ernie Kovacs Zany television and movie star, never without a cigar on the air or in films.

Duc de La Rochefoucauld-Liancourt In the oldest glorification of the cigar in the French language he got right to the point: "It raises your spirits."

Bartoleme Las Casas Chronicled the discovery of the cigar in the New World.

Rush Limbaugh Commentator, author. When his conservative political opinions are not riling leaders of the feminist movement, whom he calls "femin-nazis," his flamboyant cigar smoking is aimed at getting the smoke police's noses out of shape.

Franz Liszt Composer. He said, "A good Cuban cigar closes the door to the vulgarities of the world." So does his music.

Amy Lowell Poet, critic, author, cigar smoker.

Lyons & Burford Also known as Nick Lyons and Peter Burford, publishers of this book.

Thomas Marshall He could be the only Vice President of the United States (1913–1921) made famous by an offhand remark.

W. Somerset Maugham English author. He liked a mild cigar of delicate aroma and medium length.

Herman Melville Wrote weighty books about big men and bigger whales while smoking large cigars.

The Menendez family Legendary Havana family, makers of the Upmann and Montecristo brands.

H.L. Mencken Acerbic journalist who could find something nasty to say about almost anything, except the cigars he smoked.

Montezuma The Aztec king welcomed the *conquistadores* with the cigars used in courtly ritual. Unfortunately, his guests responded by taking over his country and doing him in.

Alfred de Musset French poet, he said cigar smoking was "the best way to kill time." He killed a lot of it in the company of George Sand, whom Davidoff called "the greatest of lady cigar smokers in history."

Aristotle Onassis Before he married Jacqueline Kennedy he was famous for his millions and a yacht equipped with a magnificently stocked humidor.

Ron Perelman Owner, Consolidated Cigar Corporation.

Prince Rainier of Monaco Few had ever heard of him until he married Grace Kelly, except for the tobacconists who kept him supplied with Chateau-Margaux and Rafael Gonzales Lonsdales.

Sir Walter Raleigh It would be cute to say that the champion of American tobacco lost his head over it, but King James I condemned him for a variety of personal grievances unrelated to tobacco.

Maurice Ravel The composer of *Bolero* and other classic works claimed smoking Havanas inspired him.

Edward G. Robinson In 1949 cigar importers named him "Mr. Cigar." Except for Al Capone, Robinson was arguably the best-known cigar-smoking gangster in America, although Robinson's bad guys were just characters in his movies.

Rothschild Banking family for whom the cigar is named.

Arthur Rubinstein Classical pianist, once owned a tobacco plantation in Cuba. His cigars had his picture on the bands.

Babe Ruth At times it seemed as if the cigar in his mouth was as big as the baseball bats that won him the title "Sultan of Swat" in the glory days of American baseball.

George Sand There is no evidence that her manly pseudonym had anything to do with her passion for cigars.

John Singer Sargent American portrait painter. When he did not have a paintbrush in hand, the man who painted the world's most famous personalities held a cigar so frequently that the right side of his mustache was the color of tobacco.

William Tecumseh Sherman Civil War general. He had his men set fire to Atlanta and other places in the Confederacy with as much zest as he lit cigars. "War," he explained, "is hell." And a good cigar was a smoke.

Harry Smith Affable host of *CBS This Morning*. Among his favorite cigars is "Oscar," the house brand of the Waldorf-Astoria's famed chef of that name.

The Governor of New York during the "Roaring Twenties" was gravel-voiced Alfred E. Smith. No public official before or since contributed more to the image of the politician as a wheeler-dealer in a "smoke filled room" than the man Smith's protégé, Franklin Delano Roosevelt, nicknamed "the happy warrior." Courtesy of New York Public Library

Joaquín Sorolla y Bastida Spanish artist. The Valencian-born painter of sun-filled scenes of women and children on Mediterranean beaches was never photographed at his easel without a lighted cigar in his lips.

Stendahl (Marie-Henri Beyle) French writer. He favored Italian-made Toscanis while writing sexy literature.

Bert Sugar Reporter and writer on the world of boxing, he adopted as his personal sartorial hallmarks a slouch-brimmed hat and a long cigar, smoked with the band on.

Mark Twain The author of *Huckleberry Finn* and *Tom Sawyer* claimed to have given up smoking cigars a thousand times. His ever-present cigar contributed to its popularity in late-nineteenth-century America. Wrote an essay in 1890 entitled "Concerning Tobacco" and insisted that smoking a cigar provided "the best of all inspirations."

Jack L. Warner One of the founders of Warner Brothers Pictures and connoisseur of Hoyo de Monterrey Panatelas. A picture of him with a cigar in hand was the stereotype of the Hollywood mogul, although Darryl Zanuck of 20th Century Fox could give him a run for his money in the mogul department.

Evelyn Waugh English author, best known to American audiences for the public television series *Brideshead Revisited,* based on his novel.

John Wayne One can only imagine what the Duke would do if he were still around and someone from the smoke police demanded he snuff out his cigar. For some of his classic western films, if the script called for him to light up, he had a supply of specially made smokes that were extra-large, in keeping with his generous physiognomy.

Virgina Woolf One thing the British novelist and essayist loved was a good cigar.

Rodrigo de Xerxes One of Columbus's adventurers, he was the first of the "discoverers" of America to light up one of the natives' cigars (October 28, 1492).

Darryl Zanuck Longtime boss of 20th Century Fox Pictures, he used some of his personal profits to ensure a steady supply of Havanas by investing in Cuban tobacco plantations.

So what is it in the cigar that has proved to be such a lure for smokers, both celebrated and not?

Few film actors could do more with a cigar to illuminate a character than Orson Welles, whether it was a newspaper titan in Citizen Kane *or a corrupt police chief in* Circle of Evil. *Welles is pictured here filming* Othello *in Safi, Morocco, 1950.*
AP/Wide World Photos

One of the most succinct explanations was the one given by David Letterman. It is the feel, the smell, the taste.

All those who have appreciated the cigar since Columbus's time have agreed. They found in the cigars cradled gently between thumb and finger a beckoning to contemplate life and in so doing engage in a singular communication with the self that Galsworthy defined as the soul.

In plumes and eddying clouds from a cigar, the poet Horace Smith found nothing less than the transience of human life:

> *Since life and the anxieties that share*
> *Our hopes and trust,*

Are smoke and dust,
Give me the smoke and dust that banish care.
I soar above
Dull earth in these ambrosial clouds like Jove,
And from my empyrean height
Look down upon the world with calm delight.

8

Good Cigars in Store

No less the true, and set aside all joke,
From oldest time he ever dealt in smoke;
Than smoke, no other long he sold, or made;
Smoke all the substance of his stock in trade;
His capital all smoke, smoke all his store,
'Twas nothing else; but lovers ask no more—
And thousands enter daily at his door.

—JACOB CATS

In the 1995 film *Smoke* the proprietor of a cigar store speaks of the location of his shop with deep affection as "my little spot."

"It's my corner, after all," Augie Wren tells one regular customer. "It's just one little part of the world. But things happen here, too, just like everywhere else."

Written by Paul Auster and directed by Wayne Wang, the film is

The 1995 film "Smoke" added to the comeback of the cigar and contributed to an upsurge in cigar smoking by women.

Courtesy of Miramax Films

set in the Brooklyn Cigar Co. in the Park Slope section of Brooklyn in present-day New York. But it could have been set at one time or another in virtually any small city, town, or village in America.

In creating the fictional store, the film's designer, Kalina Ivanov, furnished it with fixtures and props that include a sign that advises customers to RELAX, HAVE A CIGAR. Ivanov told an interviewer the desire was to evoke "layers of history, as if the store had gone from one generation to the next."

For most of the twentieth century a place just like it, plus a barbershop, drugstore, and five-and-dime, had formed both the centerpiece and the underpinnings of the commerce of the lives of ordinary people in the United States. Before cornfields and cow pastures gave way to sprawling, homogenized shopping malls, going downtown on a Saturday night meant a twenty-five-cent ticket to a movie the whole family could enjoy, a nickel Hershey bar, swing music on the jukebox with a selector in every booth in the soda shop, and a visit by "Dad," "Pop," "the breadwinner," "the old man," or whatever the head of the family was called, to the cigar store.

It was to the earliest of such emporiums, frequently set up as part of a general store, that the colorful and outlandishly attired traveling salesmen "drummed up" business for the products of the country's fledgling cigar makers. In the cases they toted from town to town were samples of the wares that, if accepted by the proprietor, would soon be on the way by parcel post.

Should the buyer hesitate in laying in a stock of whatever was being hawked, the salesman offered the enticement of "a premium." In most instances that incentive came in the form of a gratis personal supply of the smokes for the reluctant buyer. No one ever considered it a bribe or a kickback.

To assist the proprietor in enticing his customers to buy a particular product the manufacturers provided their salesmen with ornate advertising art. These colorfully lithographed posters and display boards, as well as the cigar box lids, usually depicted idyllic landscapes or portraits of contemporary celebrities. Many featured beautiful Latin American women. Almost all had on them somewhere a representation of a "gold medal" that its particular brand had been awarded for superior qualities at one exposition or another, truth or not.

"The effect on the purchaser of the massed, gaudy embellishments was, apparently, hypnotic," Jerome E. Brooks notes in *The Mighty Leaf*. "With his eyes 'glued' to the 'gorgeous' adornments he hardly knew what his groping hand found in the box and conveyed to his mouth."

Similar "art" also blossomed on the sides of barns and any other building with a large blank wall from which the landlord might pick up a little pocket money by leasing the space for advertising purposes. Eventually, cigar makers provided the store owner with a sign for the front of his establishment. Of course, the only name on the sign besides the proprietor's was the brand of the cigar maker that furnished it.

While signage was an innovation in nineteenth-century America, signs had been flourishing on tobacconists' shops in England at least as early as 1614. Ben Jonson's play *The Alchemist* in 1610 featured a "tobacco man" named Abel Dugger. It promptly became the name of several tobacco-selling establishments, including a store run by Peter Cockburn some two hundred years later. In Jonson's *Bartholomew Fair* a character named Humphrey Waspe casts aspersions on a shop named Black Boy that purveys "the scurvy, roguy tobacco." The name alludes to the association of blacks with tobacco cultivation and remained a popular name for tobacco shops well into the nineteenth century.

Other tobacco shop signs that came into wide use in Britain were, not surprisingly, SIR WALTER RALEIGH and THE VIRGINIAN. Another common name was The Tobacco Roll. A Mrs. Flight used the name in 1766 for a shop one door away from St. Christopher's Church in Threadneedle Street. Another was operated by Richard Lee around 1730. It was Ye Golden Tobacco Roll, situated in Panton Street. The sign is described in the catalog of prints and drawings in the National Collection of the British Museum as "an oblong enclosing an oval, the spandrels being occupied by leaves of the tobacco plant tied in bundles." It also depicts "several gentlemen" smoking tobacco.

One of the most popular signs to emerge over the years in Britain had as its chief feature the figure of a Scottish Highlander attired in a kilt, usually the Black Watch. This figure also manifested itself in statues of painted, carved wood standing in front of the stores. In the United States, the cigar icon was a wooden Indian.

The effigies began appearing around the middle of the nineteenth century. One theory attributes their use to widespread illiteracy. A man who couldn't read probably had heard that Indians introduced Columbus and his men to tobacco. Thus, he was assumed to be perfectly capable of associating an image of an Indian with smoking, especially if the figure held a bunch of tobacco leaves or a cigar. One of the most famous, perhaps inspired by a chief of the Iroquois, stood for many years in front of a store in Chicago. He was called "Big Chief Me-Smoke-Em" and proved sturdy enough to survive the city's most disastrous fire.

Obviously, were any such object with such a name employed in advertising today, Native Americans and civil rights groups, who allege that names and symbols of baseball and football teams such as the Atlanta Braves and the Washington Redskins are demeaning, would find it outrageous. In reality the figures of a century ago bore little, if any, resemblance to particular nations or tribes and few of them accurately reflected the attire and bodily adornments of the real people.

Many artists who carved and painted them had never laid eyes on a Native American. Consequently, they simply draped them in blankets, put feathers on their heads and moccasins on their feet and the occasional tomahawk or a bow in a hand and a quiver of arrows at the back.

Among the better and most prolific producers, with staffs of carvers working under him to meet the large demand, was Thomas Brooks. He began as an apprentice at John L. Cromwell's workshop at 419 Water Street, New York, carving emblems (usually women) for the prows of ships. He set up his own firm in 1848 along the South Street waterfront just as work in the shipbuilding yards went into a decline. But around 1855 tobacconists solicited him to supply carved figures. That change and some shrewd investing in real estate made Brooks a very wealthy man.

Samuel Anderson Robb was chief among carvers who served apprenticeships with Brooks. Encouraged by Brooks to study the fine arts, Robb went on to become Brooks's main rival and the leading carver of tobacconists' figures in America.

A contemporary writer describes the process:

> The wood used is generally white pine, which is bought in logs of various lengths. The artist begins by making the roughest kind of an outline—a mere suggestion of what the proportions of the figure are to be. The log is blocked out with the axe into appropriate spaces for the head, the body down to the waist, the portion from there to the knee, the rest of the legs (which are at once divided), and the feet. The surface of the wood soon becomes chipped up by the chisel and the log generally takes on more definite form. Then when the figure is completely evolved the finishing touches are put in with finer tools. Detached hands and arms are made separately, and joined to the body with screws. Then the various portions are appropriately painted, the whole is set on a stand running on wheels, and it is ready for delivery.

Another popular adornment for the fronts of cigar stores, especially in cities, was the policeman. This copper kept guard in 1902 at a tobacco shop on West 42nd Street between Eighth and Ninth Avenue in New York City. Courtesy of New York Public Library

One of the first of these carved figures was made for the tobacco shop of Christopher Demuth of Lancaster, Pennsylvania, in 1770. It was a "delicate Colonial gentleman" holding a snuff box.

The figure of an Indian did not appear until the 1840s. The forms ranged in dimension from life-sized for display at the front of the store to figurines for counters and window display. So lively was the market for these effigies that William Demuth & Company of New York enjoyed a brisk sideline selling them to what one of its ads called "segar stores, wine & liquors, druggists, Yankee notions, umbrellas, clothing, tea stores, theaters, gardens, banks, insurance companies &c."

Not all were made of wood. The Demuth firm also sold figures made of cast metal. If you had been around in 1890 you could have purchased one for $175. A century later, bidding for a truly fine example of the highly collectible cigar store Indian, expect to pay as much as $100,000 for a wooden one and about $50,000 for metal. (For places where they might be available, see "The Cigar Smoker's Source Guide.")

These works of art and marketing were not all perfectly erect. There was a line of what the tradesmen called "leaners." In this form the figure might rest an elbow on a tree stump, an oversized cigar, a stack of barrels, rolls, and boxes of tobacco and cigars. One made by Brooks in 1861 and sold to Philip Poss for his cigar store in Fremont, Ohio, stood in front of that establishment for more than ninety years.

Tobacconist Nat Sherman welcomed four of the Little People who portrayed Munchkins in the 1939 movie classic "The Wizard of OZ" to his famous New York City store. Courtesy of Nat Sherman

So widespread and highly regarded as art were these figures—both leaners and uprights—that when the McAlpin Hotel opened in 1912 in New York's Herald Square, an Indian was installed in the lobby. It was ultimately donated by the McAlpin to the Museum of the City of New York.

Although it was the cigar store Indian that adorned most of the stores, the carvers also made figures representing Scotland's Highlander and a variety of exotic characters in turban and fez, along with jockeys, sailors, and baseball players. At the pinnacle of fame for the opera singer Jenny Lind, effigies of "the Swedish Nightingale" graced many sidewalks.

Their placement as inducements to passersby to come into a store eventually contributed to the demise of the wooden Indians as declarations of the treasures available within. In the end the cigar store Indian proved to be a hindrance to pedestrian traffic and was supplanted by signs on storefronts like the one above the shop in the movie *Smoke*. Its big Te-Amo cigar sign holds out the promise that inside the store are newspapers, candy, film, magazines, and the most important item to the firm that supplied the sign: cigars.

History has not placed its finger on the exact spot where the first cigar store opened in the United States, but the title of "the oldest continuously operating" store is claimed by Demuth's Tobacco Shop in Lancaster, Pennsylvania. It opened for business in 1770. A few years later it sold smokes to General Edward Hand, an aide to George Washington. President James Buchanan, the only Pennsylvanian and bachelor to serve in the White House, was also a regular customer. Other venerable stores cited in research for an article by cigar historian Shandana Durrani were Iwan Ries & Company, Chicago (1857); the L.J. Peretti Company of Boston (1870) and the David P. Ehrlich Company, also in Boston (1868); Leavitt & Peirce, across the Charles River in Cambridge (1886); Straus Tobacconist, Cincinnati, Ohio (1880); W. Curtis Draper Tobacconist, Washington, D.C. (1887); Fader's in Baltimore (1891); Rich's Cigar Store, Portland, Oregon (1894); and Rubovits Cigars, Chicago (1894).

Compared with the longevity of these outlets, the Nat Sherman operation in New York City is a newcomer. He and his wife, Lautia, opened their first store in 1930. The present firm was founded in 1948. At 1400 Broadway in the heart of New York's garment district, it catered to kings and princes of the fashion industry and stars of the entertainment world.

Showbiz clients have been an integral part of day-to-day sales ever since, although the shop moved several times, first to 711 Fifth Avenue and at last to its present location, the northwest corner of Fifth Avenue and 42nd Street. Here it is just as likely to welcome scholars going to or from the massive New York Public Library across the street as celebrities in the world of entertainment.

In keeping with its New York identity, the store offers its own line of cigars with distinctly Big Apple names. Some are named for once famous Manhattan telephone exchanges: Murray Hill, Trafalgar, Oxford, Butterfield. Readers of cigar smoker John O'Hara will recall that one of his best-selling books is entitled *Butterfield 8*, later made into a film starring Elizabeth Taylor as a classy call girl and Laurence Harvey, another cigar smoker. Nat Sherman house brands also immortalize the names of legendary New York hotels: Algonquin,

During World War I, the Dunhill catalog featured "Things The Soldiers are Asking For." The firm packaged its cigars in special sealed tins for shipping to British troops in France or at sea. Alfred Dunhill Archive Collection

Vanderbilt, and Hampshire House. The "Manhattan Selection" takes names from some of the city's distinct neighborhoods: Beekman, Chelsea, Gramercy, Sutton, and Tribeca. Others in the "Gotham Selection" are identified by the street address numbers of the store's various locations: #65, #1400, #711, and #500. Carrying the New York theme further, there is "Sherman's V.I.P. Selection," named for some of the city's past movers and shakers: showmen Florenz Ziegfeld and P.T. Barnum and money magnates J.P. Morgan, John Jacob Astor, and Andrew

Carnegie. Great newspapers of the city's colorful past are remembered by cigars called Gazette, Dispatch, Telegraph, and Tribune. The store also caters to a worldwide clientele through its mail-order catalog. (For details turn to "The Cigar Smoker's Source Guide.") For many cigar smokers who visit New York City, Nat Sherman's is as much a "must see" as the Statue of Liberty and the Empire State Building.

Another New York City cigar store that could find itself a point of pilgrimage for cigar lovers is Mom's Cigars at the northwest corner of Fifth Avenue and 22nd Street (opposite the Flatiron Building). A small shop with an interesting assortment of wooden cigar store Indians, it provided much of the inspiration for Kalina Ivanov in designing the setting for *Smoke*.

At the heart of Manhattan's bustling Rockefeller Center is De La Concha Tobacconist. Between 56th and 57th Streets at 1390 Avenue of the Americas (true New Yorkers still call it Sixth Avenue), it caters to a midtown mixture of businesspeople who work in corporate offices in the surrounding skyscrapers, guests at a number of the city's deluxe hotels, art lovers on their way to or from the Museum of Modern Art on East 53rd Street, and radio and television broadcasters from CBS's stately headquarters at 52nd Street and the Avenue ("Black Rock") or NBC, located in the G.E. building (traditionalists will never stop calling it by its original name, the RCA Building) between 49th and 50th. Just west of De La Concha is CBS's Ed Sullivan Theater, home of David Letterman's *Late Show*. De La Concha also operates a store on the main-level Civic Center Shops at One Civic Center Plaza in Hartford, Connecticut.

A firm that used to be located at Rockefeller Center and now operates a few blocks away on the East Side, at 450 Park Avenue, is Alfred Dunhill. This world-renowned firm also has stores in Atlanta; Beverly Hills and Costa Mesa, California; Boston; Chicago; Dallas; Honolulu; Houston; San Francisco; Montreal and Vancouver, Canada; Seattle; San Diego; and Philadelphia.

A mainstay of the cigar in Philadelphia is Holt's Cigar Company. Its main office and the distribution center for its large catalog-sales service is at 2901 Grant Avenue. The retail store is in center city at 1522 Walnut Street. Lamenting the fact that "the shortage of premium cigars continues to be a major problem," its president, Robert G. Levin, in a letter addressed to the "Dear Valued Customers" of the retail and mail-order business, remains optimistic. He writes, "The cigar industry continues to be one of the most exciting businesses in the country."

Easily the zaniest and most interesting mail-order catalog is that of J.R. Tobacco, filled with hilarious editorial commentaries on public affairs, as well as the world of cigars.
J.R. Tobacco

The thrill of selling cigars is evident in the catalog sent out by J.R. Tobacco of America, located in Whippany, New Jersey. It is spearheaded by Lewis Rothman, who fills the firm's black-and-white, no-nonsense catalog with zesty and frequently provocative language and opinions. For a "Buy 3 get 1 free" offering of Muriel cigars he writes, "You're gonna laugh, but I *like* Muriel Coronellas. I keep 'em in my car and I kinda use 'em like a pacifier when I'm driving." Following an unsuccessful pitch for a bargain on Mexican-imported Matacans, the next ad blares, "Well folks, the deal on Matacan in the last flyer didn't do 'DIDDLY SQUAT'! So, since we have all these fresh premiums up our warehouse we're offering the exact same deal—ONLY *THIS TIME* you get *two* of these gifts FREE!" The gifts were playing cards and coasters featuring paintings of Christopher Columbus's ships. The ad then warns that "unless you buy these cigars, you WILL have to see this ad over and over and over again."

A page offering a bargain price for Santa Clara 1830 cigars states, "Phooey, ANOTHER Mexican cigar!" The copy continues that what is needed is "another whole bunch of countries making cigars 'cause I've reached the limit of what I can write about Honduras, the Dominican Republic. . . . I wish Cuban cigars would become legal . . . not 'cause I think they're so great, but just because I'd have another country to write about."

On the subject of Fidel Castro, he claims to have once sold the Cuban dictator a box of La Corona Coronas. This occurred during Castro's stormy first visit to the United Nations when he moved out of a swanky midtown hotel and into the decidedly downscale Hotel Theresa in Harlem. Rothman recalls:

> My dad had a United Cigar store on 125th Street and 7th Avenue. He [Castro] came into our store all dressed up in combat clothes. Anyway, all we had in those days were green [candela] cigars, 'cause that's what Americans used to smoke, and the best of them were Corona Coronas . . . 3 for a buck. He bought a whole box. Frankly, I didn't know who the hell he was. I only knew he spent over 15 bucks on cigars in one shot.

A controversial topic covered in another issue of the J-R flyers is the North American Free Trade Agreement (NAFTA), which is denounced because "our politicians don't know zilch about the Mexicans and all the underhanded crap that goes on down there." In a pitch for another brand of "cheap" cigars the copy wishes that the government would stop issuing guidelines and warnings about health hazards in foods. "They wanna protect us," it says, "like we're really too stupid to know that a double cheeseburger and french fries are not quite as healthy as a bowl of gruel. Why don't they protect us against the REAL important stuff like 'some assembly required.'"

That the J.R. "catalog" is entertaining is certified by a subscriber who wrote to Rothman complaining that the latest edition had been loaned to a pal and "now he won't give it back."

Lucky New Yorkers do not have to order from J.R. through the catalog. The firm operates what it claims is "the world's largest cigar store" on East 45th Street with row after row of shelves abrim with what appears to be every brand in the world.

Another major purveyor of cigars through mail order is the Thompson Company of Tampa, Florida. Pointing out that the firm has been in existence since 1915, its chief executive, Tom Timmins, states, "We're no Johnny-come-lately." Crammed with various bargains on cigars, the catalog also offers a huge variety of items unrelated to cigars, from an array of pipes and cigarettes to a reproduction of the Colt six-gun carried by cowboys, a "John Wayne belt buckle," and a genuine Irish shillelagh. The company does not operate a store.

Although shopping by catalog is now a major component of life in the United States, there will always be cigar smokers who prefer the experience of buying their favorite brands in a place where the proprietor or clerk stands ready to offer counsel to a beginner buying cigars one at a time and conviviality to the connoisseur who takes them home in anticipation of the moment when he will, as Kipling lovingly declared, "Open the old cigar box."

The Cigar Box

Tradition credits the introduction of the cigar box to the English banking firm of H. Upmann and dates it to 1830. For the use of the bank's directors in London, Havanas were packed and sealed in cedar boxes that were stamped with the bank's emblem. Prior to this innovation cigars had been sold in bundles wrapped with pigs' bladders. To deal with the odor, pods of vanilla were inserted. No such additive was needed for the cedar containers. Indeed, cedar boxes eventually ended the general custom of bundling cigars into "wheels" and tying them with ribbon. While bundled cigars are still available, the boxed cigar is now the industry norm. Although cardboard is widely used to make boxes, cedar remains the standard for boxing premium cigars.

Boxing cigars and standards for the number of cigars per box are the result of a decree by President Abraham Lincoln. Because the Union was strapped for cash to run the war, the Revenue Act of 1864 and a modification of it the following year required that all cigars, whether domestic or imported, be packed in wooden boxes of 25, 50, 100, or 250 and that they carry a federal tax stamp to be sold legally.

The inspiration to decorate the outside of the boxes has been attributed to Ramon Allones. A Galician immigrant to Cuba, he started making his own brand of cigar and in 1837 began to identify his product through the use of colorful lithographed labels on the boxes. Other makers quickly adopted the practice. This inevitably led to the development of a new market for artists and a boon to others whose bent was to the crasser arts of selling through creative advertising.

Then, as today, these individuals were usually men and then, as now, they believed that there could be no surer way to sell a product to a man than with an advertisement extolling the beauty of a woman. For a man's product that was made in Cuba (reportedly by young women who actually turned the tobacco leaves into cigars by rolling them on their thighs!), what better image on a box of Havanas could there be than that of a voluptuous Latin girl?

To attract men who might not be quite so lascivious (or at least unwilling to appear so, even in a cigar store), artists of the cigar box had a variety of more sedate subjects that were no less appealing to the masculine nature. Labels offered flags, war heroes and statesmen, racehorses, dogs, guns, athletes, and men engaged in plain honest work. In the explosion of industrial development and national expansion following the Civil War, the decorations included the romance of the railroads and hardy men of the western frontier towns known as cowboys. With the debut of the automobile, label artists lost no time in recognizing that it was an object that men were bound to fall in love with.

"In the golden age of cigar label art," writes Joe Davidson in his massive book on collecting, *The Art of the Cigar Label,* "literally thousands of subjects were used to attract the eyes and nickels of our forefathers. Since most cigars were smoked by men, it is no surprise that the various themes shown on the labels were what the lithographers thought men liked."

Like the cigar store Indian, cigar box art is eagerly sought by collectors. Among this group of avid seekers is cigar industry historian Tony Hyman. The author of *Handbook of American Cigar Labels* and contributor of an article, "Four-Square Masterpieces," in a 1994 edition of *CIGAR Aficionado,* he notes, "Boxes and labels once displayed in elegant panoramas designed to entice your dimes and quarters are now recognized as the first, finest and most varied point-of-sale advertising in history."

To differentiate among brands, makers also came up with another idea.

The Cigar Band

The inspiration to wrap a band around a cigar has been attributed to Gustave Bock. Born in the Netherlands, he was one of the first Europeans to settle in Cuba and helped to develop its cigar industry in the nineteenth century. When boxes and their enticing labels were coming into popularity, he sought to distinguish his brand from the many others on the market. His idea for the small paper band for identification also served to secure wrapper leaf that at times had the unhappy habit of coming loose.

Another theory concerning the advantages of a band holds that it keeps a smoker's fingers from staining, not insignificant in an era when gentlemen's evening wear included white gloves. But historian Tony Hyman scoffs at this notion. A cigar is not grasped at the location of the band, he points out, adding that paintings, drawings, and photographs of dandified gents of the age when the well-dressed man

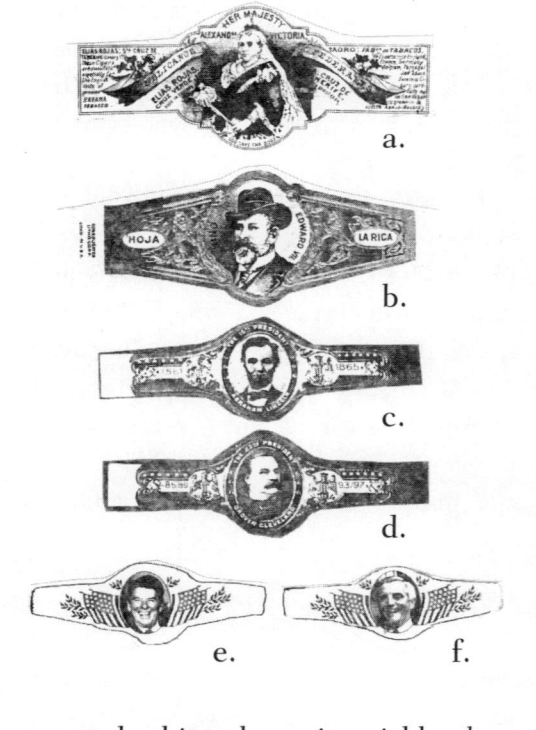

a.

b.

c.

d.

e.   f.

Cigar Bands:

*(a) Britain's Queen Victoria's oppo-
sition to smoking did not keep cigar
maker Elias Rojas from naming
one of his products after her. (b)
When Victoria's son became King
Edward VII, he lifted the ban on
cigar at Buckingham Palace with
the words, "Gentlemen, you may
smoke." (c and d) Among presi-
dents of the United States honored
on cigar bands were Abraham
Lincoln and Grover Cleveland. (e
and f) During the 1980 presidential
election, the campaigns of both
President Ronald Reagan and
his Democratic opponent, Vice
President Walter Mondale, handed out cigar with bands featuring
pictures of the candidates.*

Courtesy of New York Public Library

sported white gloves invariably show the men *without* their gloves
while smoking.

Whatever reason impelled Bock to put bands on his cigars in the
1830s, it was an idea that caught fire. By 1855 most cigars had them.
The impetus for bands stemmed, as well, from the obvious success of
labels on boxes in separating one brand of cigar from another and, it
was hoped, engendering brand loyalty. Just as box labels gave a lot of
work to artists, the arrival of the cigar band loosed a flood of designs.
Naturally, they also joined box art in the hearts of hobbyists and collectors everywhere.

Rather than discard a band, some individuals who might have
regarded collecting them as unmanly found they still had a use, as

Hemingway did in presenting one to Ava Gardner as a forget-me-not. Others who were just as romantic but in a financial pinch entered the folklore of the cigar by way of slipping a band onto the ring finger, left hand, until money for a proper engagement ring was found.

As discussed earlier, whether to leave the band on a cigar while smoking can bring on heated debate. Old etiquette books call for removal. But much of the old etiquette has gone the way of men's white gloves, leaving the issue of "on or off" up to the individual. Now, when people have no problem walking around in clothing emblazoned with the name and/or logo of the designer, there would appear to be no grounds for insisting that the cigar smoker desist from advertising the brand of cigar he prefers by taking off the band.

As to the preference of the authors of this book, Gordon is "on" and Jeffers is "off." Gordon, an artist, is also a collector of bands. However, he has not yet gone so far in his painting as has one New York artist.

The wife of a cigar smoker, painter Beth Fidoten in 1995 had a show at a Manhattan smoking club (Cigar Bar) of her efforts to celebrate cigars. In watercolor and pen and ink she depicted all kinds of cigars in works titled *Monte Cristo Habana, Dunhill With Tube, Zen of the Cigar, Davidoff With Box,* and *Culebras Twisted Cigar.* The inspiration to feature cigars came, she said, when she found one of her husband's cigar boxes stored in the refrigerator.

"I became fascinated by the simple shape and colors," she told a newspaper reporter who covered her exhibition, "as well as the different bands and labels, with the gold that sets them off. Now I go searching for the unusual."

People without that talent could display examples of the artistry of cigar boxes on T-shirts. A 1995 catalog of the Casual Living company of Tampa, Florida, offered (not surprisingly) a choice of shirts with colorful reproductions of the White Ash and Paid in Full brands. The shirts cost $25 each, plus shipping, and were sent in actual cigar boxes.

Makers of Macanudo cigars have embraced the idea of advertising their product by way of clothing. The firm offers a line of jackets, caps, and other apparel with the Macanudo logo prominently displayed.

A catalog of the Thompson Cigar Company offers a "smokers get outta my face" T-shirt depicting one of cartoonist Jeff MacNelly's tree-top birds with a cigar in its beak and the words "Thanks for not bitching." He is shown leaning nonchalantly but defiantly against a sign with a red ring with a cigarette in the center and a red slash—the universal "no smoking" symbol.

Thus far, today's incarnations of King James I have not intruded into the sanctum of the cigar store in the way animal rights activists have stormed into furriers' salons and splashed paint and even blood on women who had the bad luck to cross their paths on the sidewalk. However, if history has demonstrated that the past is prologue, it should be noted that during King James's reign an antismoking subject of the realm was within his rights to accost a smoker and knock the pipe or cigar out of the hand or mouth of the "offender."

Kindred Spirits

Yet I know five or six
Smokers, who freely mix
with their neighbors.

—C.S. CALVERLY

I n the years since a small group of cigar lovers gathered in a hotel in Laguna Niguel, California, under the auspices of the charity honoring Milton Berle's late wife, Ruth, similar convocations have blossomed like spring flowers from coast to coast.

At once a celebration of the cigar and a means for makers of premium brands to proselytize on behalf of their products, these highly publicized events were also analyzed by commentators on the present social scene as representing the "angry white male" syndrome. It was as if cigarists had belatedly rallied to the cry of Peter Finch (a cigar smoker on the movie screen and off) as the television news anchorman in cigar-smoking playwright Paddy Chayefsky's 1976 film *Network* demands that members of his TV audience stick their heads out their windows and yell, "I'm mad as hell and I'm not going to take it anymore."

Whether angry over the depredations of the smoke police or simply curious, what might either a veteran or a novice cigar smoker expect to find and do if he or she shells out the cost of a ticket to one of the extravaganzas billed as a "Big Smoke"?

Waiting for the doors of the grand ballroom of a swank hotel to swing open, a cigar devotee may well appreciate how a child feels while clutching an "E" ticket before the portals of Disney World. But, as in that world of innocent make-believe, a couple of hours at a Big Smoke are likely to turn out to have been spent waiting on crowded lines ending in exhaustion and crankiness. The adult who has forked over well over a hundred bucks and invested time and effort attending a Big Smoke may reap an experience that is memorable not for its sensory delights but for tramped-on feet in a room so packed with people that New Year's Eve in Times Square seems tranquil in comparison.

The entry fee entitles you to a book of coupons, which, when presented at the booths of top-of-the-line cigar makers, gets you a "free" cigar and a chance to consort with hundreds of men (and a few women) drawn, like yourself, by the prospects of the genteel companionship associated with smoking a good cigar. Under the spell of such high expectations, and with promotional tote bags filled with the freebies, no one seems to realize that the admission fee could have easily bought a box of fine cigars to be savored during many quiet evenings at home with feet up and a snifter of brandy at hand, blissfully alone.

But it is not only the lure of gratis cigars that brings you and the others into this maelstrom. You've also come for the free food, and, indeed, it's there. Mixed with the spice of the blue cigar smoke wafts the tantalizing aroma of superb cuisine presented by four-star, cigar-friendly restaurants. In tempting array are the appetizers, main courses, and desserts of gourmet chefs—if you can make it through the throngs of the hungry who truly believe there is such a thing as a free meal. Although the quality of the food proves generally outstanding, finding a place actually to sit and enjoy the repast can be a daunting experience resulting in a severe case of agita, and the realization, in retrospect, that going after the food and cigars of a Big Smoke is not an undertaking for the faint of heart.

But the movement to restore the cigar to its proper place in society can be more than a clever enterprise of shrewd merchants of premium cigars and the inventor of Big Smokes, Marvin Shanken. Hundreds of "cigar evenings" have been held in scores of cities and towns without all the hustle and an outlay of a lot of money. Away from the glare of television news cameras hungering for shots of the rich and famous for the eleven o'clock news, these sociable gatherings built around the cigar are organized by individuals and groups with nothing more on their agenda than enjoying and sharing the companionship of the cigar.

Another manifestation of the need for the long-harried cigar smoker to find kindred souls is the cigar club. Typical of these members-only groups in 1995 are the Caribou Club of Aspen, Colorado; the Private Smoking Club in Cincinnati, Ohio; The Cigar Connoisseurs of Chicago and the Cigar Connoisseur Club in New York City; Cigar Club at Town Point, Norfolk, Virginia; Les Amis de Cigar/George Sand Society of Santa Monica, California; and the Cigar Society at Florida State University in Tallahassee.

There may be similar clubs in your community. Ask about them at your cigar store.

Restaurants

As newspaper columnist Art Buchwald warned diners in the nation's capital, lighting up a cigar in a restaurant nowadays could be hazardous. In numerous locales new laws and pressure from antismoking activists have limited after-dinner smoking of all kinds. Therefore, before you make a reservation or follow a maître d' to a table, ask what the smoking policy is.

In New York City the city council has enacted a complicated statute regarding smoking in restaurants. Although the prudent fancier of an after-dinner cigar should inquire when making reservations as to what is permitted, data on cigar-friendly eateries may be found in *The Insider's Guide to Smoking and Dining in Manhattan,* by Carol Davenport. Published by Kato Enterprises, it is available in bookstores or ordered by calling 1-800-95-GUIDE. Similar guides may be available in other cities. Inquire at your tobacconist or a bookstore. A national listing has been published by *CIGAR Aficionado* and should be available in most cigar stores.

As discussed earlier, the nation's capital became a focus of those in the antismoking movement who would impose their views on everyone by statute, edict, or ruling by federal regulatory bodies, such as the Food and Drug Administration's scheme to declare nicotine a hazardous substance in the same category as hard drugs. However, the cigar-smoking movers and shakers of the legislative, executive, and judicial branches of the government could still find amenable places to dine, drink, and smoke. Among them, the Capital Grille was described in a front page article in the Style section of the *Washington Post* as an "upscale eatery on lower Pennsylvania Avenue offering thick steaks, fat cigars and sanctuary for happy capitalists. . . . The very act of walking in the door has a defiant edge, a swagger of deregulated power. Political correctness is incorrect. . . . Waiters serve up the 24-ounce porterhouse (House Speaker Newt Gingrich's favorite) followed by *crème brûlée,* port and Davidoff cigars."

Other places in the capital with a reputation as "in" spots for a power lunch or dinner include Duke Zeibert's, the Jockey Club at the Ritz-Carlton, and the John Hay Room in the historic Hay Adams Hotel, opposite the smokeless, large white mansion at 1600 Pennsylvania Avenue.

The Cigar Smoker's Source Guide

A lurch to starboard, one to port
Now forward, boys, go we
With a haul and "Ho" and a "That's your sort!"
To find out Tobac-kee.

"The Discovery of Tobacco, a sailor's version,"
in *Cigar Tobacco World*, London, 1895

For further information on particular brands of cigars and makers of related products mentioned in this book, you may find the addresses on the following pages helpful.

CIGARS

CIGARS OF HONDURAS, INC.
Suite 166
3101 New Mexico Avenue NW
Washington, DC 20016

CONSOLIDATED CIGAR CORPORATION
5900 North Andrews Avenue
Fort Lauderdale, FL 33309-7098

CUESTA-REY INTERNATIONAL
PO Box 2030
Tampa, FL 33601

DE LA CONCHA TOBACCONIST
1390 Avenue of the Americas
New York, NY 10019

ALFRED DUNHILL
450 Park Avenue
New York, NY 10022
For other stores in Atlanta, Beverly Hills, Boston, Chicago, Costa Mesa, Dallas, Honolulu, Houston, Montreal, Philadelphia, San Francisco, Vancouver, Seattle, and San Diego, consult the telephone book or directory assistance or dial 1-800-776-4053.

GOLD LEAF TOBACCO COMPANY
550 Secaucus Road
Secaucus, NJ 07094

HINDS BROTHERS TOBACCO LTD.
96–185 Carlton Street
Winnipeg, Manitoba, Canada R3C 3J1

HOLT'S CIGAR COMPANY
1522 Walnut Street
Philadelphia, PA 19102

J.R. TOBACCO OF AMERICA
301 Route 10 East
Whippany, NJ 07981

LANE LIMITED
2280 Mountain Industrial Boulevard
Tucker, GA 30084

LOS LIBERTADORES
1826 Ponce de Leon
Suite 281
Coral Gables, FL 33134

M & N CIGAR MANUFACTURERS, INC.
PO Box 2030
Tampa, FL 33601

MIAMI CIGAR & CO.
7476 NW Eighth Street
Miami, FL 33126

NAT SHERMAN
500 Fifth Avenue
New York, NY 10110

SANTA CLARA, NA, INC.
1515 East Broad Street
Statesville, NC 28677

SAVINELLI ELR
PO Box 526
Morrisville, NC 27560

SWISHER INTERNATIONAL, INC.
PO Box 2230
Jacksonville, FL 32203

TABACALERA A. FUENTE Y CIA.
Santiago
Republica Dominicana

THOMPSON CIGAR COMPANY
5401 Hanger Court
Tampa, FL 33634

TINDER BOX INTERNATIONAL CORPORATE OFFICE
1 Bala Place East, Ste. 102
Bala Cynwyd, PA 19004
(800) 846-3372

VILLAZON & CO., INC.
25 Park Way
Upper Saddle River, NJ 07458

CHINCHALES

ANTELO CIGARS
437 West 17th Avenue
Miami, FL

BOQUILLA
2116 Summit Avenue
Union City, NJ

CHAVELO CIGARS
7345 West Flagler Street
Miami, FL

EL CANELO CIGAR FACTORY
709 NW 27th Avenue
Miami, FL

LA ISLA
505 42nd Street
Union City, NJ

LA PLATA CIGARS
1026 South Grand Avenue
Los Angeles, CA

MOORE & BODE
810 West 16th Avenue
Miami, FL

RODRIGUEZ & MENENDEZ
4321 Armenia Avenue
Tampa, FL

VINCENT & TAMPA CIGAR CO.
2503 21st Street
Tampa, FL

ACCESSORIES

ASPREY *(all kinds)*
725 Fifth Avenue
New York, NY 10022

BOSTON CIGAR CUTTER COMPANY
(cutters)
10 Phoenix Row
Haverhill, MA 01832

HINDS BROTHERS TOBACCO LTD.
(humidors)
96–185 Carlton Street
Winnipeg, Manitoba, Canada R3C 3J1

ZIPPO MANUFACTURING COMPANY
(lighters, collector's guide)
33 Barbour Street
Bradford, PA 16701

CIGAR STORE INDIANS

MARK GOLDMAN, HOUSE OF OXFORD
172 Fifth Avenue
New York, NY 10010

HILL GALLERY
163 Townsend Street
Birmingham, MI 48009

ALAN KATZ AMERICANA
175 Ansonia Road
Woodbridge, CT 06525

STEVE MILLER
17 East 96th Street
New York, NY 10128

LIGHTER CLUBS

On the Lighter Side
International Lighter Collectors
PO Box 536
Quitman, TX 78783

Pocket Lighter Preservation
Guild
11220 West Florissant, #400
Florissant, MO 63033

CIGAR CLUBS

Clubs are forming everywhere. Consult your cigar dealer for those in your community. If there isn't one in yours, start one.

HISTORIC CIGAR STORES

Demuth's Tobacco Shop
114 East King Street
Lancaster, PA 17602

W. Curtis Draper Tobacconist
604 14th Street NW
Washington, DC 20005

David P. Ehrlich Co.
32 Tremont Street
Boston, MA 02108

A. Fader & Son
107 East Baltimore Street
Baltimore, MD 21202

Leavitt & Peirce
1316 Massachusetts Avenue
Cambridge, MA 02138

L.J. Peretti Company, Inc.
2$^{1}/_{2}$ Park Square
Boston, MA 02116

Rich's Cigar Store
801 SW Alder Street
Portland, OR 97205

Iwan Ries & Co.
19 South Wabash Avenue
Chicago, IL 60603

Rubovits Cigars
320 South LaSalle Street
Chicago, IL 60604

Nat Sherman
500 Fifth Avenue
New York, NY 10110

Straus Tobacconist
410–412 Walnut Street
Cincinnati, OH 45202

CIGAR RETAILERS

It is impossible to list all of the cigar retailers in North America, even all of the first-rate ones. We have, however, put together a list of stores that you may find helpful if you are in one of the major metropolitan areas in the United States.

Baltimore

A. Fader & Son
107 East Baltimore Street
Baltimore, MD 21202
(410) 685-5511

Boston

L.J. PERETTI CO.
2 1/2 Park Square
Boston, MA 02116
(617) 482-0218

Chicago

AROUND THE WORLD
1044 West Chicago Avenue
Chicago, IL 60657
(312) 327-2343

IWAN RIES & CO.
19 South Wabash Avenue
Chicago, IL 60603
(312) 372-1306

RUBOVITS CIGARS
320 South LaSalle Street
Chicago, IL 60604
(312) 939-3780

UP DOWN TOBACCO
1550 North Wells Street
Chicago, IL 60610
(312) 337-8505

Cleveland

DAD'S SMOKE SHOP
17112 Lorain Avenue
Cleveland, OH 44111
(216) 671-3663

Columbus

HUMIDOR PLUS
6157 Cleveland Avenue
Columbus, OH 43231
(614) 891-9483

PIPES & PLEASURES
4244 East Main Street
Columbus, OH 43213
(614) 235-6422

Dallas/Fort Worth

EDWARD'S PIPE & CIGAR
3307 Oak Lawn Avenue
Dallas, TX 75219
(214) 522-1880

LONE STAR CIGAR, INC.
13305 Montfort Drive
Dallas, TX 75240
(214) 392-4427

SMOKES ETC!!
3014 Alta-Mere Drive
Fort Worth, TX 76116
(817) 244-9394

Detroit

HILL & HILL TOBACCONISTS, LTD.
2001 Renaissance Center
Tower 200, Level 2
Detroit, MI 48243
(313) 259-3388

El Paso

PAPA'S
6315 North Mesa
El Paso, TX 79912
(915) 585-8965

Houston

THE BRIAR SHOPPE
6366 Richmond Avenue
Houston, TX 77005
(713) 529-6347

JEFFERY STONE LTD.
9694 Westheimer
Houston, TX 77063
(713) 783-3555

Indianapolis

HARDWICKE'S PIPE & TOBACCO
743 Broad Ripple Avenue
Indianapolis, IN 46220
(317) 257-5915
(downtown) 24 North Meridian
Indianapolis, IN 46204
(317) 635-7884

TOBACCO OUTLET
8613 North Michigan Road
Indianapolis, IN 46268
(317) 334-9700

Jacksonville

EDWARD'S PIPE & TOBACCO
5566-23 Ft. Caroline Road
Jacksonville, FL 32277
(904) 745-6368

Los Angeles

CIGAR JOINT
7153 Beverly Boulevard
Los Angeles, CA 90036
(213) 930-2341

THE SMOKING SECTION
7801 Melrose Avenue, Unit #4
Los Angeles, CA 90046
(213) 653-0328

Memphis

THE TOBACCO BOWL
152 Madison Avenue
Memphis, TN 38103
(901) 525-2310

Milwaukee

UHLE'S PIPE SHOP
114 W. Wisconsin Avenue
Milwaukee, WI 53203
(414) 273-6665

Nashville

UPTOWNS SMOKE SHOP
3900 Hillsboro Road
Nashville, TN 37215
(615) 292-6866

New Orleans

THE EPITOME
729 St. Louis
New Orleans, LA 70130
(504) 523-2844

New York

ALFRED DUNHILL O FLONDON
450 Park Avenue
New York, NY 10022
(212) 753-9292

MOM'S CIGARS
32 West 22nd Street
New York, NY 10010
(212) 924-0907

NAT SHERMAN
500 5th Avenue
New York, NY 10010
(800) 692-4427

Philadelphia

CHESTNUT SMOKE SHOP
27 South 8th Street
Philadelphia, PA 19106
(215) 923-1699

BLACK CAT CIGARS
1518 Sansom Street
Philadelphia, PA 19102
(215) 563-9850

Phoenix

CHRISTOPHER'S
2398 East Camelback Road, Suite 290
Phoenix, AZ 85016
(602) 957-3214

STAG TOBACCONIST
132 Park Central Mall
Phoenix, AZ 85013
(602) 265-2748

San Antonio

TOBACCO BOWL OF TEXAS
622 NW Loop 410, Suite 276
San Antonio, TX 78216
(210) 349-7708

San Diego

FUMAR CIGAR
1165-A Garnet
San Deigo, CA 92101
(619) 270-9227

SMOKER'S LAND
13295 Black Mountain Road
San Deigo, CA 92129
(619) 484-7373

San Francisco

GRANT'S PIPE SHOP
562 Market Street
San Francisco, CA 94104
(415) 981-1000

SHERLOCK'S HAVEN
1 Embarcadero Center
San Francisco, CA 94111
(415) 362-1405

San Jose

MISSION PIPE SHOP
812 Town & Country Drive
San Jose, CA 95128
(408) 241-8868

Seattle

ARCADE SMOKE SHOP
610 Pine Street
Seattle, WA 98101
(206) 587-0159

NICKEL CIGAR
89 Yesler Way
Seattle, WA 98104
(206) 622-3204

Washington, DC

GEORGETOWN TOBACCO
3144 M Street NW
Washington, DC 20001

W. CURTIS DRAPER
640 14th NW
Washington, DC 20005
(202) 638-2555

MAGAZINES

CIGAR Aficionado
387 Park Avenue South
New York, NY 10016

The Cigar Monthly
1223 Wilshire Boulevard
Suite 241
Santa Monica, CA 90403

Smoke Magazine
Lockwood Trade Journals
130 West 42nd Street
New York, NY 10036

Further Reading

I HAVE BEEN GUILTY OF SEVERAL MONOGRAPHS. HERE,
FOR EXAMPLE, IS ONE, 'UPON THE DISTINCTION BETWEEN
THE ASHES OF THE VARIOUS TOBACCOS.' IN IT I ENUMERATE
A HUNDRED AND FORTY FORMS OF CIGAR, CIGARETTE, AND
PIPE TOBACCO, WITH COLOURED PLATES ILLUSTRATING
THE DIFFERENT ASH.
—*Sherlock Holmes*

One of the surprises that greeted us while conducting research for this book is the lack of other works on the particular subject of the cigar and regarding smoking in general, except a flood of negative writings triggered by the Surgeon General's 1964 report on smoking and health. The few positive books on the cigar that have found their way into print and libraries have been quite recent.

The Cigar Companion, BY ANWER BATI
(Running Press, Philadelphia, PA).

The Connoisseur's Book of the Cigar, BY ZINO DAVIDOFF
(McGraw-Hill, New York).

The Art of the Cigar Label, BY JOE DAVIDSON
(The Wellfleet Press, Edison, NJ).

The Ultimate Cigar Book, BY RICHARD C. HACKER
(Autumngold Publishing, Beverly Hills, CA).

Handbook of American Cigar Boxes, BY TONY HYMAN
(Treasure Hunt Books, Pismo Beach, CA).

The Illustrated History of Cigars, BY BERNARD LEROY AND
MAURICE STEFAN
(Harold Starke, Ltd., London).

Perelman's Pocket Cyclopedia of Cigars, COMPILED BY RICHARD
B. PERELMAN
(Perelman Pioneer & Company, Los Angeles, CA).

A much earlier volume dealing with the overall history of tobacco is *The Mighty Leaf,* by Jerome E. Brooks (Little, Brown and Company, Boston, MA.

Also available from the publisher of *CIGAR Aficionado* are the "Buying Guide to Premium Cigars" and the "Guide to Cigar Friendly Restaurants." The quarterly magazine's offices are at 387 Park Avenue South, New York, NY 10016.

Further historical information regarding cigar boxes and bands is available from Tobacciana Research and Resources, PO Box 3028, Pismo Beach, CA 93448.

The most enchanting source of material relating to the cigar, containing much of the poetry quoted herein, is a little book, *Pipe and Pouch, the Smoker's Own Book of Poetry,* compiled and published by Joseph Knight Company, Boston, in 1895. In its pages we found the perfect way to end ours:

My Last Cigar

'Twas off the blue Canary Isles
A glorious summer day,
I sat upon the quarter deck,
And whiffed my cares away;
And as the volumed smoke arose,
Like incense in the air,
I breathed a sigh to think, in sooth,
It was my last cigar.
I watched the ashes as it came
Fast drawing to the end;
I watched it as a friend would watch
Beside a dying friend;
But still the flame swept slowly on;
It vanished into air;
I threw it from me,—spare the tale,—
It was my last cigar.
I've seen the land of all I love
Fade in the distance dim;
I've watched above the blighted heart,
Where once proud hope hath been;
But I've never known a sorrow
That could with that compare,
When off the blue Canaries
I smoked my last cigar.

— JOSEPH WARREN FABENS

The Language of Cigars

BINDER Leaf that holds the cigar together.

BULK A pile of tobacco leaves left to generate heat (known as "sweating").

BUNCHING Combining of filler and binder leaves in preparation for rolling into wrapper leaf.

CAP Covering of the end of the cigar's head.

CHAVETTE Trimming knife used in manufacturing process.

CHURCHILL Long, straight cigar with medium to thick body.

CLARO A pale brown cigar wrapper leaf (also called NATURAL).

COHIBA Cuban tobacco and a prized brand of Cuban cigars.

COLORADO Reddish dark brown wrapper leaf.

CORONA A thick cigar with a straight body.

CULEBRA A cigar with a twisted or braided body.

CUTTER A device for clipping the head of cigar; also known as a GUILLOTINE.

E.M.S. English Market Selection. Rich brown wrapper traditionally preferred by cigar smokers in the United Kingdom.

FERMENTING The aging of tobacco leaves.

FILLER The inside leaves of a cigar.

FOOT The end of a cigar that is lighted.

HAND Leaves of similar color, usually twenty, tied at the bottom of their stems during the fermenting process.

HANDMADE A cigar bunched and rolled entirely by hand. Also known as HAND-ROLLED.

HAVANA (Habana). A Cuban cigar.

HEAD The part of the cigar that gets clipped and goes in the mouth.

HECHO A MANO Spanish for a cigar that is partly handmade.

HECHO TOTALMENTE A MANO Spanish for completely handmade cigar.

HUMIDOR Wooden box with built-in humidifier for storing cigars.

LONSDALE A long cigar with medium to thick ring gauge.

MACHINE-MADE Mass-produced cigars made entirely by machinery.

MADURO Very dark wrapper leaf.

MARRYING One of the latter stages in the making of cigars in which they are stored, usually in cedar-lined rooms at a constant humidity, to allow the flavors of the component tobaccos to blend. Also called AGING.

OSCURO Black wrapper leaf.

PANATELA Slender cigar with tapered body.

PREMIUM CIGAR A handmade cigar.

PURO A Cuban cigar made for the export market. Also a cigar whose ingredients (filler, binder, and wrapper) are grown in the same country.

RING GAUGE The thickness of a cigar measured in increments of $1/64$ inch.

ROBUSTO Short, thick cigar with straight body.

SHADE Tobacco leaves grown beneath coverings (usually linen); also refers to wrapper leaves grown in the Connecticut River Valley (Connecticut Shade).

STOGY A generic term for a long, thin (usually cheap) cigar; named for the cigars made in the same area of Pennsylvania that produced the Conestoga wagon.

VEGA Cuban tobacco plantation.

VUELTA ABAJO Tobacco-growing region at the western end of Cuba that produces the prized "Havana" cigars for world export.

WRAPPER The outer leaf.

INDEX